Let Your 'no' Mean "NO."

~ * ~

Learning To Get Along In Community and Make It Work

by

Emily Windsor-Cragg, BS, MA

Lake County California
March 2016

PROLOGUE

In community we want to feel heard and empowered. We want our dreams to be do-able and possible. . . . Looking at the seas, forests and meadows, Diversity rules. No one specie dominates; and when one group gets too large, it wrecks everything. So too with Society. There is no One Way Deal. We the diverse human family must learn how to get along in the world and with each other. This book explores ideas, how to garner, finance, barter and cooperate. It's supposed to be fun, but this is not gospel, just taking a stab at it. Indeed, if we can conceive of Peace, we can build it, stone-on-stone, step-by-step, crop-by-crop and year-by-year . . . with God's help.

TABLE OF CONTENTS

~*~ *INSPIRATION* ~*~

"I made thee that thou shouldst receive inspiration, not only from the world external to thyself, but inspiration from the members of thy body. My impression upon thee is inspiration; but thou must realize My inspiration, in order to know Me. An idiot holdeth fire in his hand, and it giveth him pain, but yet, he knoweth not the cause, nor whence the origin of the pain. So, also, I come to thee, and give thee inspiration, but thou discernest not Me. Another man discerneth My Presence, and My inspiration. He heareth Me speak; he seeth My Person. Yet, I am with both alike. One man openeth his mouth to speak, and behold, My words come forth. And yet another saith: No man know Jehovih; none have heard Him. One man is sensitive, as a plate for a picture, and he catcheth My Light instantly, and knoweth it is from Me. Another one saith: A sudden thought struck me! But he discernest not whence it came. ***OAHSPE,*** Book of Inspiration, Ch. III, v. 14-23.

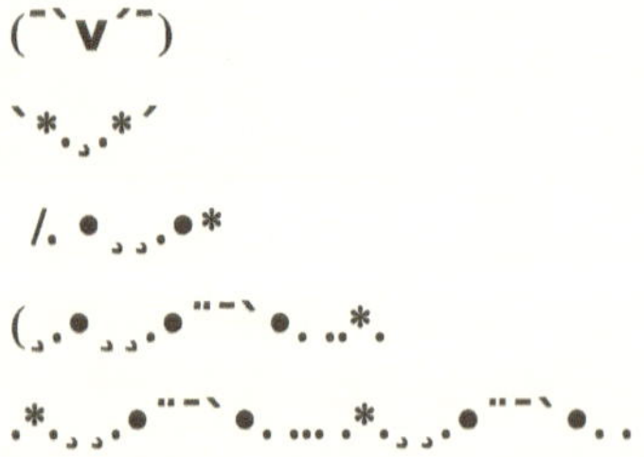

INTRODUCTION

Leading a Movement to
Gather a Community Hierarchy :

There are FOUR LEVELS of the Etherworld guiding Leaders in 3rd Density Physical existence, in which and where Laws of Cause and Effects precede Manifestations.

---ONE---There's an External Hierarchy incarnate (human remnant-Annunaki) for each community leadership : these are skilled technicians who judge and declare what can become eternal "good effects," for lacking waste, want or suffering.

---TWO---There are personal Networks of Souls : Bloodlines, Friendships, Families, Angelic Corps : Watchers who see what happens, without judging, but these experience and articulate what is true and what is not true to life, for confronting and addressing.

---THREE---There are corps of Angels, Saints and Spirits who can eneable or disable, evoke or intrude upon, initiate or block mental thoughts and constructs; human-Etheric ("teams") outside Hierarchy, doing special projects, like me, myself inspired as an Inquisitor to question and place in jeopardy what does not work out due to Injustice or Unfairness, lacking mercy, so that questioning, repulsing and toppling bad ideas is the work, and Hate, treachery, selfishness and deceit cam be toppled by those people who >see< that what is true and useful is being suppressed. ~Remember~

---FOUR---Humanity is not alone confronting ET's and Galactic Hierarchies. There is one Creator God, YHVH, who assembled this Earth long ago, who wrote the code to human DNA and who developed classical music, Who deals with Life in response to prayer of the people : a Source Life Carrier Who encourages repulsing error and Who helps make what can become eternal, permanent.

~~Emily Windsor-Cragg

FINANCING -:- By Holy Law

SEED MONEY : Working the Law of Tenfold Return

By

Jon P. Speller, D.D., 1965
John Hoshor, D.D.

Edited and appended by Emily Cragg
Lake County California
2004-2016

~*~ ~*~ ~*~

Within the last fifty years many thousands of people have read John Hoshor's wonderful, SEED MONEY: THE LAW OF TENFOLD RETURN AND HOW IT WORKS. They have grasped the scientific principle behind the Seed Money Formula and have successfully applied it in their daily lives to end their money troubles. Others have not, for various reasons. This book is to help people get to prosperity, who didn't get it the first time.

John Hoshor wrote [in a booklet published by the Church of Religious Science] : "Let us imagine that we have $50 in U.S. currency. We could put the money in a savings bank and it would return us approximately $2 a year. We could buy a mortgage certificate and get a return of $3 or even $4 a year. Or we might use the money to buy a share or, depending on the price, several shares of stock in some corporation, perhaps get dividends and, provided we bought at the right time and sold at the right time, make a profit on the transaction."

"Of course, we could also use the $50 for food, rent, clothing, books, tools or for other needs or just for pleasure. . . . That is why money is the medium of exchange. It can be used for many things."

"One of the things for which money can be used--which at this writing is not generally known--is as SEED MONEY. This means that we can so use money that we reap a harvest of multiplied money."

Here are a few of the blocks that some people have had using the Seed Money Principle.

A retired man called me long-distance from California. He said that he has read SEED MONEY, followed the formula faithfully, but could not get a return. It seemed that his greatest joy in retirement was driving his car on vacation. One day the old car just gave out--it couldn't go another mile and it had to be towed to a wrecking yard. For two months the man tried to use Seed Money to demonstrate enough money to buy a new car. He gave his Seed Money to his Church, believing he would get a tenfold return. But nothing happened.

He seemed to understand the principle clearly and to have complete faith in its workings. He puzzled me for a while. Then he said, "I better hang up. The call costs too much filthy money."

I asked, "Why do you say that money is filthy?"

His reply gave me the answer to his failure to receive his tenfold return: "Isn't money the root of all evil?" [1 Tim 6:10] he asked.

I told him: "The Bible doesn't say that 'money is the root of all evil.' It says, 'the love of money is the root of all evil,' and even that needs explanation. In Biblical days money as we know it today was very seldom used. Most exchanges were on the barter system. A carpenter would exchange a table for some bushes of grapes. A farmer would exchange grain for clothing, and so on. Money, in gold and silver, was only used for large transactions.

Today money is a universal medium of exchange for all goods and services. When we fix it firmly in our minds that the service that money provides is different from the love of gain, profit and advantage, then we can positively view money as a tool, not as a goad or something to hoard.

The Bible says you 'cannot serve God and mammon.' [Luke 16:13] Mammon represents hoarded money--that which is not placed into circulation. Money in circulation is God in action. Money which is hoarded is useless, for money is merely the medium of exchange.

I said to the man who called me, "You have had a hatred of money because you thought it was evil. Since like attracts like, you have attracted the hatred of money back to you, returned you no good even for the good you have done."

“Don't think of money as a dead object of greed. Think of it as a living means of acquiring your needs--good for yourself and for others. Right now, money should represent for you the car that will give you mobility and options--both of which are good."

He thanked me and two weeks later I heard from him again. "It's marvelous," he said with great joy in his voice. "I received my tenfold return. Yesterday my married daughter drove up from Los Angeles in her Volkswagen. She gave me the keys, telling me that her husband just bought her a new station wagon so that they and their children could go on camping trips in the mountains. She knew that my old car had given out, so insted of selling the Volkswagen, she gave it to me."

"Wonderful," I said.

"You know," he said, "once I realized that it wasn't money for money's sake that I wanted but the good I could buy with it, I overcame that mental block. The Volkswagen is worth even more than ten times my Seed Money, and on top of that it doesn't use as much as as my old car--I can travel much farther for the same money."

This is just one illustration how a person's changing their concept of money enables the use of the Seed Money Principle.

Every creative act begins with a thought. Have you been thinking of money as evil? Or, have you been thinking of money as the good that it represents and manifests in your life?

John Hoshor wrote: "Just how do we plant seed money? What happens when we do plant it? . . . We give it to our Church or to a hospital, school or college or to any of the Social Service organizations which subsist on donations. Or, if we wo wish, we could give it to any needy person, friend or stranger."

Then we follow a specific mental formula derived from the Great Teacher aqnd proven absolutely true and dependable by such financial giants as the first John D. Rockefeller, Andrew Carnegie, Julius Rosenwald, Andrew Mellon and others of great wealth."

"With perfect safety, without any risk whatever, our seed money so planted will return to us tenfold. We will receive back $500."

The second block often found in people who

have not yet succeeded in practicing the Principle of Seed Money is this: many people don't understand how the giving of Seed Money produces its tenfold return without any risk whatever.

But it is a fact. The Law of Tenfold Return always works. There is absolutely no risk whatever in the Principle of Seed Money. If you do not follow the formula precisely, there is risk, but then you are not actually practicing the Principle.

I received a rather irate letter from an airplane stewardess flying on charter flights out of Chicago. She wrote: "Mr. Hoshor's Seed Money doesn't work. I know because I tried it. When I fly to Las Vegas I play the slot machines. Sometimes I win. With Seed Money I don't get back a dime."

Writing back to her I gently informed her that the Seed Money Principle itself always works but that she apparently is not really practicing it.

As illustration I wrote that the Principle of the Parachute is itself infallible. A properly made, properly packed, properly checked, and properly used parachute never fails to open.

If the parachute is not made properly, is not packed properly, is not checked properly or is not used properly it will not open. That is not the fault of the Principle of the Parachute or of the parachute itself. It is the fault of the persons or persons who made, packed, checked or used the parachute.

The Principle of Seed Money works in the same way as the Principle of the Parachute, or as any other

Principle, for that matter. If the Principle isn't properly applied you aren't working the Principle.

The Seed Money Principle is not a gamble such a slot machine or a lottery. When you think that you may get your tenfold return from "planting" some Seed Money -- you won't. When you believe that you will get a tenfold return on your Seed Money, you will.

Jesus said, "What things soever ye desire, when ye pray, believe that ye receive them, and ye shall have them." [Mark 11:24] He did not say that you won't have them. He did not say that you might have them. He said that you shall have them.

The "magic" word Jesus used there is "believe." There is no room for chance in believing. There is no room for chance in the Law of Tenfold Return.

I advised the stewardess to only practice Seed Money when she felt that she could remove all doubts about receiving her return. If she couldn't try to remove her doubts about receiving her return. If she couldn't try to remove her doubts, I advised her to forget it.

Two months later I received another letter from the stewardess. She said that her reason for wanting her tenfold return was because she wished to have enough money to visit her fiance at the US Air Force at Wiesbaden, Germany. As a non-scheduled domestic airline stewardess she didn't get reduced fares which most airline employees have. She said that with one week's meditation on the Principle of Seed Money--after she had received my letter--she had become convinced that the Law of Tenfold Return worked in Principle and that she could apply that to attain her desired trip. She gave ten dollars, following the formula properly in every step, to her Church that Sunday. On the following Wednesday she received an offer to take the place of a MATS (Military Air Transportation Service) stewardess on a European flight--to Wiesbaden Germany.

Her tenfold return? She called her parents to tell them of her new assignment. Her father told her that he had just received the return of his income tax overpayments. He sent her a gift of one hundred dollars for extra spending money.

This is just one example of many deserving people who give, and give, and give Seed Money, without really believing they will ever get their return. They don't, until they really believe that they will.

Do you think that you only may get your tenfold return? Or do you believe that you will get your tenfold return?

Some people have the same problem the stewardess had, but in a different way. They give their Seed Money to their church, believing they will receive their return. Then a member of their family, a friend, a co-worker or some other person scoffs at their belief. Doubt creeps in. Their return is deflected, and the Law appears not to work.

John Hoshor writes: "Can't you just see the bankers and the economists holding up their hands in horror at Seed Money? They will tell you it's impossible!"

"You are welcome to believe them and lay this booklet aside or give it to someone else. Or you can read it and learn how SEED MONEY multiplies, why it multiplies and by following the principles and methods set forth, prove its truth and worth for yourself.

"Incidentally, it has often been said, many times inaptly, that 'The truth shall make you free.' The only truth that will make you free is the truth that you prove for yourself. If you cannot prove something in your own experience--if you cannot apply it and demonstrate it in your daily life--whatever truth it is, or is not, will not make you free."

A housewife visited me with the complaint that her husband didn't believe that the Seed Money Principle really works. "He laughs and calls it a fool's gimmick," she said, "he keeps me from receiving my tenfold return."

I told her, "No one can prevent you from receiving your tenfold return except you yourself. Your husband's remarks cannot prevent your tenfold return unless you yourself give them the permission and power to do so."

As Ernest Holmes wrote in his great book, THE SCIENCE OF MIND, "Nothing can happen to us unless is happens through us. That which we refuse to accept to us cannot be, and that which to us 'is' cannot help becoming a reality in our lives."

I asked her to remove the blocks caused by her acceptance of her husband's remarks by denying they had any effect on her exercise of the infallible Principle of Seed Money. I asked her to affirm that she, and she alone, puts the Power and Abundance of the Universe into motion for her tenfold return.

I asked her, recognizing her great faith in the promises of the Scriptures, to recite--as an addition to the Seed Money process--when giving her Seed Money: "Surely, blessing I will bless thee, and multiplying I will multiply thee." [Hebrews 6:14] So God promised. So is it with Tenfold Return."

Six weeks later the housewife paid me another visit. She was now practicing the Law of Tenfold Return successfully. There was an interesting sequel. Her husband, seeing his wife's success with Seed Money--despite his scoffing--secretly started applying the Seed Money Principle himself. He finally, rather sheepishly told his wife, "It works." And it does work.

The Law of Tenfold Return does not only work here and now, but forevermore in the future. The Law of Tenfold Return has always worked throughout the ages. John Hoshor writes:

"Long ago the prophet Malachi knew about SEED MONEY. A prophet becomes a prophet because he is inspired to rise to higher levels than most people and thus can more clearly see things and know things for what they really are."

Malachi said: "Bring ye all the tithes into the storehouse, that there may be meat in mine house, and prove me now herewith, saith the LORD of hosts, if I will not open you the windows of heaven, and pour you out a blessing, that there shall not be room enough to receive it."

In present day words Malachi's inspired statement means that you should give your Seed Money to your Church so that, as you freely give, so you shall freely receive. And it will be proved NOW, declares the Law of Tenfold Return, that the horn of Infinite Plenty shall be opened and pour you such an Overflowing Abundance of Good that you shall not have room enough to consume it.

A man I know is in the printing business. He was one of the printers of John Hoshor's SEED MONEY. His business had taken a turn for the worse. His printing presses were idle more often than they were busy. His overhead—rent, payroll, utilities, etc.--was pushing him deeper and deeper into debt.

He asked me, "Does Seed Money really work?" I told him, "Of course--when you follow the process faithfully, the Law of Tenfold Return always works. It's simple CAUSE and EFFECT."

"But can I receive as much as I need?" he asked.

“Nothing can limit what you receive except for the limits you place on yourself," I replied, "do you know the Twenty-Third Psalm?"

"Yes," he said.

I counseled, "Then remember David's words: "Thou preparest a table before me in the presence of mine enemies; though anointest my head with oil; my cup runneth over.' [Psalm 23:5] It doesn't say could runneth; it says runneth Isn't that definite? It doesn't say half full. It doesn't say full. It says runneth over. Isn't more than enough, enough?"

"Yes," the printer said. I could see that he understood. Several months later I called him to order another five thousand copies of SEED MONEY.

He said, "My business is running at more than capacity. Even with overtime I can't keep up with the demand. Thanks to Seed Money. But I'll print the books for you and Seed Money the overtime charges."

This printer is now so prosperous that he spends three months of every year in Florida--thanks to his understanding and practicing of the principle of Seed Money.

Do you demonstrate ten times one dollar, but fail at ten times ten dollars or ten times one hundred dollars? Or, do you know that the Law of Tenfold Return works equally well on a thousand dollars as it does on a single dollar?

The only limitation on your return is caused by yourself. As Dr. Raymond Charles Barker of First Church of Religious Science in New York City says: "All causation is from your subconscious mind, and your subconscious mind can be changed. You are the only one who can change it."

You alone can affect your reaping of your tenfold harvest--regardless of the amount of cash, valuables or skill-effort involved, [by changing your behavior].

As John Hoshor says, "Were Malachi around today to witness for us he would tell you that our $50 planted as SEED MONEY and properly cultivated would certainly return us $500 and that other seed money sums would return proportional harvests." Jesus, too, was focused on seeding change, giving, giving, giving; and He knew what the outcome would be.

As money is solely a medium of exchange, your tenfold return is not necessarily in the form of currency. John Hoshor cited how a friend of his proved Malachi's promise--Malachi 3:10--with [an example of, of all things] typewriters:

"My friend Sigmund was studying to be a writer. He felt that he could progress faster if he had a typewriter. Sigmund asked me to help him demonstrate a typewriter. I agreed and we started to work that night.

"Although Sigmund had often been writing at his desk when his landlady came to straighten up the apartment, the very next morning she suggested that he go to the basement and get the typewriter some folks who had once lived there had left. She told Sigmund that he might have the typewriter.

"Sigmund phoned that day and gave me an account of what had happened. He said, however, that the machine was not new and that he had taken it to have it cleaned and put in working order.

"The following day Sigmund picked up the typewriter and asked me to come and see it. I went to his place. I'm quite certain that it was not the first typewriter ever manufactured, but it could have been the second. The two of us sat quietly and looked at it.

"'Does it work?'" I asked him.

"Sigmund laughed and said, 'It does, in a manner of speaking.'"

“During the next few weeks the machine needed fixing several times and Sigmund told me that he had finally decided to leave it in the repair shop.

"Soon after I was called to Phoenix, Arizona where I spent several months. When I returned to California I went again to see Sigmund.

“He asked, 'Why don't we try the typewriter demonstration again?'"

"'What kind of machine do you want?'"

"Sigmund thought and answered, 'It doesn't have to be new but it should be a late model of a standard make and also be in good working condition.'

"I said, 'All right, that's our pattern, a late model standard make in perfect working order.'

"We both went to work on it that night.

"It was three days before I spoke with Sigmund again. He phoned and said that he had tried to reach me the day before. I explained that I had been away on a business appointment and asked what happened.

"Sigmund said, 'A friend of mine who's been drafted into the Army brought me a typewroter that is only three months old. I once lent him my car to drive his mother to Seattle and he said he didn't know when he'd need the typewriter again, if ever, and he wanted me to have it."

"I asked, 'What kind of condition is it in?'

"'Perfect,' was Sigmund's answer.

"I said, 'Fine.'

"Sigmund said, 'That's not all. You remember my telling you about my friends who live across the street?'

"'The ones for whom you mowed the lawn when the man had his ankle broken?' I asked.

'The same. When I came back from the store this afternoon, Mary--she's the wife--called me over. They are going back East and have more than they can haul in their car. They bought a typewriter a couple of years ago when they tried out the mail order business at home, but the business didn't prosper so they gave me the machine. Mary said that they had been watching me writing in longhand at my window and they wanted me to have it. I couldn't refuse, so I brought it home.

"I said, 'Great. Is it in good condition too?'

"Sigmund said that it was in perfect condition. Then I pointed out to him that we had demonstrated two typewriters. I heard him laughing over the phone.

"I asked, 'What are you laughing about?'

"He answered, 'I have three. This morning when I went for the mail there was an almost new machine in front of my apartment door with a typewritten note--This is a gift--I thought that perhaps you had sent it.'

"I told him, and I told him truthfully, 'Sigmund, not only did I not send it, I know nothing at all about it.'

"Sigmund said, 'We'd better turn it off. I don't want to go into the typewriter business.'

"Since those years Sigmund has used the formula time and again and is today a prosperous writer and lecturer on the subject."

The demonstration of Sigmund's typewriters is an illustration of but one of many articles of value received in accordance with the Law of Tenfold Return.

When my wife was approaching the time of the birth of our first child, we moved from Manhattan to an apartment in Kew Gardens. Our child was still to be delivered in the hospital in Manhattan where we had already made arrangements.

It was a wintry January in New York, and we didn't have a car. We applied the Law of Tenfold Return to demonstrate transportation for the day when our baby would arrive.

Although on the day when my wife had to go to the hospital the weather was so bad that that most people could not find a taxi--we had not one, not two, but three vehicles to take us to the hospital.

Leo and Olga, a couple we know, were there with their car. Another friend, Pete, dropped by with his car. And a taxi I had called also arrived.

I gave the taxi to some people who couldn't locate a cab. The taxi-driver was surprised when I put a dollar in his hand anyway. He didn't know that it was Seed Money.

Olga and Leo drove us to the hospital in Manhattan. Pete asked if he could drive my wife and the baby back to Queens on the day when they would be released from the hospital. Little did he know that the ten dollars in taxi fares which he would save us represented tenfold return of the dollar I had given to the driver of the taxicab.

The day came when my wife and new baby daughter were released from the hospital. It was also the day after a big snow-storm. Pete's car was snowed under--we had no shovel to dig out the wheels.

I started an Affirmation. I had hardly finished when seemingly from nowhere a very small boy carrying a very large shovel appeared. He had been shoveling sidewalks and had noticed our plight. In no time the car was free from the snow and ice and we were on our way to Manhattan.

The Law of Tenfold Return can fulfill every desire. It is not limited by price. It is not limited by lack. As John Hoshor wrote:

"The resources of the Infinite are Infinite, and every human being [--human being defined as a physical will directed by an Infinite Spirit--] has direct access to these resources.

"Jesus knew about SEED MONEY and how to multiply it. He referred to it more than a few times and with the loaves and fishes demonstrated it with great success before a huge throng of people. [Each person receiving a piece of fish or loaf broke off a small piece and passed the remainder on.]

"In the parable of the talents Jesus told about three men. One had been given one talent, another had been given two talents and the third had been given five talents.

“A Roman talent was a denomination of money approximately equivalent to $500 [in U.S. 1960's currency].

"The man who had the two talents doubled his, as did the man who had the five talents. They were each commended and promised: 'Thou has been faithful over a few things, I will make thee ruler over many things' [Matt 25:21 & 23].

In effect, this was saying that the principle they had applied could be used over and over again ad infinitum, that it was Unlimited in its operation.

"The man who had one talent did not multiply it but instead buried it in the ground. He was reprimanded and told that his one talent would be taken from him.

"Use part of your money as SEED MONEY and you will become prosperous--enough."

In the parable of the talents Jesus illustrated why many people fail even today in their attempts to practice the Principle of Seed Money.

The man with the one talent--who failed to increase it—explained: "I was afraid, and went and his thy talent in the earth."

Many people who sometimes attempt to work the Law of Tenfold Return fail through fear--created and perpetuated only by themselves. The Law of Tenfold Return is only the orderly working of God in our minds, our bodies, and our affairs. In United States dollar bills is written, "IN GOD WE TRUST"--very good advice.

Those who do not receive their tenfold return because of fear that it will be lost, lose their money as surely as the man who buried his talent in the ground ultimately lost his [to God's Judgment that he manifest

NO TRUST]. In trusting God one cannot fear--and the Principle of Seed Money demands absolute trust in God--Omniscience, Omnipotence, Omnipresence.

A doctor wrote to me that he could see the scientific basis of the Principle of Seed Money in harmony with the fundamental One Law of the Universe--but he couldn't overcome the gnawing fear that his Seed Money would be lost.

I wrote him what Job had said: "For the thing which I greatly feared is come upon me, and that which I was afraid of is come unto me" [Job 3:25].

I told him that the Law of Tenfold Return knows no evil. If one fears that he will lose what he has, he will surely lose what he has, for his thoughts of fear express what he wants.

The doctor realized the boomerang caused by his fear--one that had cost him not only his tenfold return, but had caused him a tenfold loss. He saw the truth in Jesus' words: "For unto every one that hath shall be given, and he shall have abundance: but from him that hath not shall be taken away even that which he hath" [Matt 25:29].

Today the doctor has banished the word "fear" from his vocabulary. By the Principle of Seed Money he has built up a flourishing and satisfying practice. He gives a copy of SEED MONEY to every new patient.

John Hoshor put it: "Fail to use money as SEED MONEY and you will remain or become needy. Why? Because the needs of Life are forever eating up your Substance, your earnings, your capital. These must be constantly replenished and extended--renewed--just as you have to forever renew your Breath of Life.

"A very small percentage of our population today uses the Law of Seed Money in one form or another. These are the rich, and especially, the very rich. Yet, perhaps one in ten thousand of these few uses the Seed Money Principle consciously, knowing what they are doing. The others have conditioned themselves to follow certain business practices, some of which are not contrary to the Law of Seed Money and which, part of the time at least, are harmonious with that Law. Their financial success is in direct proportion to how closely they follow that Law.

"It should go without saying that success will be greater where one practices the Seed Money principle consciously and constantly than where one uses it only spasmodically and accidentally."

"A typical business operation in harmony with The Law of SEED MONEY might be as follows: A man gets an idea for a new product which will confer benefit upon those who buy it. He takes the idea to a friend. They study it and agree that people will buy it and be pleased with having and using it. They also agree it will require X dollars to develop and market the product. They calculate that they can sell the item in volume and estimate that they can profit to the extent of ten times the X dollars they must invest in it. So they go into business, follow their agreed-upon course and make the profit.

"Details will differ in every case but the foregoing operational procedure is that utilized in almost every successful business venture."

A man telephoned from the South. He said that he was down to his last two hundred dollars. The only other thing he owned was some worthless land on the outskirts of his town. He had no prospects of any income.

I told him that "the earth is full of the goodness of the Lord" [Psalm 33:5]. This doesn't mean that the earth is empty of good, nor only half full of good. It means that the earth is full of good.

When you have a full dozen eggs you don't have six, you don't eleven--you have twelve, the full dozen. Our good is exactly the same. With God there is no short-changing.

But your supply is only equal to your demand, and it is up to you to make your own demand on the Infinite. There is no lack of supply, only a lack of demand. You have to claim what you want, not what you don't want.

When you plant your Seed Money and claim "weeds"--you can't expect to receive a harvest of abundance of anything but "weeds."

A little tree in Canada serves as a fine example.

The Jack Pine was once a "weed." It was not only too small to use for lumber, but a substance within its cellular structure prevented its use for pulp in the manufacture of paper. Jack Pine was considered a "true weed," with little present value and none foreseeable.

Millions of acres of Jack Pine were considered wasteland--an area larger than the State of Connecticut.

But men of a paper company in Michigan believed "that a weed is merely a plant for which man has not yet found a use." They did what others considered impossible. They found an economical way to remove the substance contained in Jack Pine's cellular structure which had prevented its use for paper pulp.

As a result, this firm is now making a beautiful, high-quality paper out of Jack Pine--employing many thousands of working people in this work.

Those who claimed nothing from Jack Pine--received nothing. Those who planted their seeds, believing in their own success--reaped the harvest.

I told the Southerner that he must not try to select a specific channel for the transmission of his return to him, that correct use of the Seed Money formula leaves the means of providing the tenfold return to its ultimate source, God.

As Eric Butterworth of the Unity Center in New York affirms in his book, "Unity, A Quest for Truth": "God is my All-Sufficient Resource. He is my Instant, Constant and Abundant Supply."

Dr. Butterworth explains: "God is my supply, everywhere evenly present, and as immediately available as the air I breathe. The moment a need arises in my life, God's infinite substance is immediately at hand to fill it. I am a child of God, and it is right and good that I manifest abundance. As God's child, I have been given the wisdom and intelligence to bring into expression all that is needed for my well-being and comfort. God inspires me with good judgment in handling the supply that is already mine, and opens the way to greater good, greater blessings, greater opportunities."

I asked the Southerner to reflect on this when he wondered about the source of his tenfold return. He promised to do so.

Nearly a month later I heard from him again. The Sunday after I had talked with him he had given a check for his entire two hundred dollars to a home for orphans, absolutely sure of his tenfold return because he was following the command to care for the orphaned and poor.

The next day he was visited by a newcomer to town. The newcomer told him that the town needed a driving range for its many avid golfers. He told the Southerner that his "worthless" land on the outskirts of town was ideal for that purpose. He offered to lease the property, put up the capital to build the driving range, and pay him a percentage of the gross receipts.

The Southerner received a down payment of two thousand dollars—ten times his gift--and subsequently will make a comfortable living from his share of the proceeds from the driving range so long as he continues to provide SEED MONEY in his community.

His prosperity is only a very small sample of what can be received through the practice of the Principle of Seed Money. The Law of Tenfold Return can make you, as it says in the line from the song,

Pennies From Heaven--"as rich as Rockefeller." John Hoshor wrote:

"The greatest fortune the world ever saw until recently in private hands was amassed by a man who thoroughly knew, understood and constantly used the Law of Seed Money.

"The first John D. Rockefeller, through his long life, put his full trust in that Law. Whether in his early days when he gave frugally but regularly to his Church or in his middle and later years when his foundations were giving many millions to better the world, Rockefeller always envisioned the many times multiplication of his gifts returning to him.

"And they did. How they did.

"Rockefeller knew the truth of the early Biblical promise, 'all the land thou seest shall be yours.' He laid his claim on the Infinite and accepted possession. It came to him. The Law always works; it's just people who fail to apply it, that fail.

Rockefeller kept his secret a secret. He taught only his family, and the Principle of Seed Money is still working full time for those Rockefellers who apply it.

The world regarded the elder Rockefeller's practice of giving a new dime to everyone he met as a rich man's idiosyncrasy, but to Rockefeller it was a deeply religious and significant act, each gift another opportunity to multiply his return. Selfish? Greedy? Do not believe it. Here was a man in love with the Law, thoroughly and all-absorbingly in love with the Law. He embraced the Law and it gave, flooding Abundance over him almost beyond human power to count. [Notice, Bill Gates operates similarly--giving huge amounts away as seed money constantly--to restore his supply, at last count, 42 BILLION.]

"Van Loon in his Life of Rembrandt paints a scene where the bailiffs are moving out the artist's stove and other furniture. In one carner of the hut his wife is lying on a pallet of straw dying of consumption [tuberculosis]. And what is Rembrandt doing? Standing in another corner of the hut painting. As Rembrandt was in love with painting, the first John D. was in love with making the Law of Seed Money work for him.

History has recorded John D. Rockefeller's practice of Seed Money, which he started at the earliest age. Before he had reached twenty-one he was giving $18.00 per month to his church--out of a salary of only $35.00 per week.

John D. Rockefeller, Jr., gave us an affirmation of his father's adherence to the Law: "I have been brought up to believe, and the conviction only grows upon me, that giving ought to be entered into in just the same careful way as investing."

He also revealed that his family did not accumulate its vast wealth for purely money's sake--a negation of the Law--for "Money itself is lifeless, impotent, sterile . . . but man with his brain, brawn and imagination, using money as servant, may feed the hungry, cure the diseased, make the desert places bloom and bring beauty into life."

If the magnitude of one's Seed Money gifts barely covers one's necessities, then an acceptance of relative poverty and simplicity can outfit a person uncumbered by possessions. There is no reason to judge a person, whether they choose to accumulate goodness or serve and work personally without accumulating anything. This is a choice God gives to us all. But at least, what is encumbent on us all is to realize that we do have that choice--how much we desire to claim against God's Abundance--that we choose to be responsible FOR, husband and steward. Rockefeller Jr. said, respecting the responsibilities his family had undertaken:

"I believe in an all-wise and all-loving God, named by whatever name, and that the individual's highest fulfillment, greatest happiness and widest usefulness are found in living in harmony with His Will."

Wealth manifests more than mere good: it extends and expands Progress with new problems, new situations, new relationships. Wealth pushes society in new directions--yes, some of which are evil, exploitative, corrupted. But without individuals who do demonstrate abundance, little new knowledge is yielded out of experience. So, God allows Wealth. It broadens experiences; yields new discoveries; subsidizes new specialties.

John Hoshor cites other notable large-scale beneficiaries of the Law of Tenfold Return:

"Andrew Carnegie, Julius Rosenwald and Andrew Mellon all knew the Law of Seed Money and practiced it throughout long and extremely prosperous lives. Not only did the gifts of these men enrich the entire world of their day, but they also multiplied personal wealth and opportunities of many others--because each of them personally learned how to claim the multiplied return of his gifts, and constantly did so claim."

We realize, they became rich and over-encumbered with possessions at great danger to their souls. Let the reader use wisdom and see that extreme behaviors produce extreme outcomes. Rich men are not known for either speaking Truth nor accepting the harness of Law. They backslide.

It was Andrew Carnegie who revealed that the truly great fortunes were not received through the worship of money for money's sake. He said that there is "no idol more debasing than the worship of money." Andrew Carnegie gave and received in his lifetime [1835-1919] $350,000,000, today the equivalent of $35 billion.

It was Julius Rosenwalk who revealed that the truly great fortunes were not received through hoarding, but through circulating money--giving money freely and receiving back whatever came. He said: "I believe that under no circumstances should funds be held in perpetuity." Julius Rosenwald gave and received in his lifetime [1862-1932] more than $60,000,000 [today: $6 billion or more].

Andrew Mellon [1855-1937], although he was a public figure—he served for a time as U.S. Secretary of the Treasury--was one of the most secretive of the great practitioners of the Principle of Seed Money. He knew that no thoughts of others could possibly get into his mind to interrupt his application of the Law if no one knew of his system to multiply his wealth. Thus, Andrew Mellon burned the notes of small debtors at Christmastime and gave away his money in large bundles with the greatest of secrecy. It is said that he gave and received in his lifetime in excess of one billion dollars [equivalent to 100 billion today].

Some of the money these very wealthy practitioners of the Principle of Seed Money gave was in the form of the Biblical tithe. But the bulk of the money given was not ten percent of what had long been received--but ten percent of what was actually received in the consciousness of these men. That was how the money multiplied, through these men's growing understanding of, "whatsoever a man soweth, that shall he also reap," the better as well as the bitter.

Money isn't >ALL< that is reaped. Neither is "nice things." Relationships are embraced or shunned, by giving or not giving: of hospitality, acknowledgment and recognition, of positive expectations or negative expectations.

Hospitality [receiving strangers and kinsmen] is the entire basis for prosperity in many cultures down through time--especially in the East. Inclusiveness and exclusiveness bear large price-tags in terms of "returning good" or "returning retribution." Remember, the Law of Ten is not limited to "money."

It encompasses all forms of openness and acceptance and Truth and honesty and generosity.

Six hundred years before Jesus' Great Ministry, the Buddha in India also taught among his sayings: "As we sow, so shall we reap." This Law, unlike the customary or usual Tithe, is not restricted in its Universality nor cultural application. Desert nomads and Inuit tribespeople depend on the Law of Ten applied to hospitality, for their very survival.

John Hoshor says of the Tithe, "Practically everyone knows about the tithe. The tithe meant that one-tenth of the person's income belonged to the Church. It was, in effect, a payment due--a thanks-giving. More than a few are reported to have used the tithe and to have become highly prosperous doing so--in Calvinistic Churches. [Calvinists came and come to RELY on their prosperity as a sign of acceptance by God in the Judgment Day scenario--a serious error].

Having faith in Prosperity is not the same as submitting to the disciplines of Sacrifices-in-Trust that Jesus taught. So, be cautious in applying this Law, lest you be stumbled by mere Materialism, Elitism or a desire for Power, all of which are very different from simply "demonstrating sufficiency" before God.

"There is a distinct difference between the Tithe and Seed Money. The Title is a gift after you have made the income. Seed Money is a gift in order to claim a tenfold return. Seed Money applies the Law directly, and therefore, much more effectively. In utilizing the Seed Money Principle you are saying in effect: 'Here's the SEED I plant. Here's the investment I make with God. Here's the money with which I bless my fellow beings. I claim my tenfold return. I am drawing on my Unlimited account with the Infinite.'"

An elderly lady asked me, "Why do I have to run so hard to stay in the same place? I've given my tithe for forty years."

I told her that many people have become prosperous through use of the Tithe--but generally through their conscious understanding of its direct effect on their financial well-being. I suggested that she continued her tithing, but add recognition that as she freely gives, so shall she freely receive. I gave her a copy of SEED MONEY.

The Seed Money Principle changed this lady's life. She grasped it with the greatest of ease. Now she circulates an ever-increasing amount of money in her life. She not only helps many people--but at the same time she now can afford many luxuries she had once denied herself.

Another man I know was up to his ears in debt. He never seemed to be able to catch up with his bills. I showed him these passages in SEED MONEY:

"Paying debts is one of the primary requisites to becoming prosperous. Some may think that they can achieve prosperity by never paying anyone. This is contrary to the Law and simply will not work. Something for nothing is always nothing. You must either pay as you go or pay later with interest compounded. . . . The best practice for prosperity is to pay your debts before they are due, insofar as it is possible, and so keep them out of your consciousness."

The man said, "That's very true--but I'm in a situation where that amounts to advice to close the barn door after the cow has been taken. I sow my Seed Money, but the only return I've been getting is more harassment from my creditors."

I told him that apparently his resentments toward his creditors and inner guilt were blocking his tenfold return. Resentment is the same as a boulder blocking a highway--if you don't remove the boulder once and for all, it will roll back and impede your way again. The prophet Jeremiah recorded this wonderful statement: "I will forgive their iniquity, and I will remember their sin no more. You must forgive your creditors and forget their resentments toward them.

And it is also important that you forgive yourself--you cannot really forgive others without forgiving yourself. Nor can you really forgive yourself without forgiving others. The Lord's Prayer makes this very clear: "And forgive us our sins [or debts] as we forgive those that sin [or are indebted] against us [Jer. 31:34; Luke 11:4].

This man gradually understood the message. He has cast aside resentment toward his creditors; he has ceased his self-condemnation. Now, through the Law of Tenfold Return, he is almost completely out of debt [because he sat down and worked out a way to settle or pay off his debts that was agreeable to everyone].

Because of his great need, this man had asked: "Why can't I demonstrate more than ten times my Seed Money?"

I read to him from John Hoshor's SEED MONEY: "Why tenfold and not elevenfold or twenty-fold or thirty-fivefold or a millionfold? . . . Simply because the number 10 is the easiest of all to multiply by. You merely add a zero to the figure with which you begin. The zero is symbolic, meaning that it is nothing to the Infinite to send you your multiplied return that to the Infinite is less than the air you breathe."

"Why not a millionfold?"

"Because you must be able to conceive yourself as having the amount you claim. In fact, you must imagine that you already have it.

"Let us say we plant--give--$50 in accordance with the Law of Seed Money and lay our claim on the Infinite for $50,000,000 in return. Then we begin to wonder where all that money is coming from. We begin to doubt. The doubt shuts off our return, creates a block. It will be the doubt that we demonstrate, not the cash. So the proper method is to start the process of giving--planting--but plant no more than you can conceive yourself as receiving in return tenfold. Then lay positive claim to that much, and only that much."

This man come to understand the answer to his question from that. Others needed a more detailed explanation.

One such young man said: "The Law knows no limitation. If I can visualize one hundred or one thousand or one millionfold return on my Seed Money, why can't I do it?"

I answered, "If you can visualize such a return--and hold it unwaveringly--you can do it. Jesus said: "If you have faith, and doubt not, ye shall not only do this which is done to the fig tree, but also if ye shall say unto this mountain, Be thou removed, and be thou cast into the sea; it shall be done' [Matt 21:21]. If any doubt seeps into your fath in your return, it will not come."

A Tenfold Return is a demonstration within the consciousness of practically everyone. For example, most people can conceive of having ten times as much money as they now have in their pocket. Most people also have difficulty in conceiving of a greater multiplication at one time. There is where doubt arises. One can reach the same goal progressively--without the strain which causes doubt.

Surely it is possible to demonstrate a larger than tenfold return. But keep in mind that even Jesus, the Christ Spirit incarnate, did not walk on water all the time. In this way the young man learned the hidden wisdom in moderation and realistic goals.

A young lady had a more basic problem--one which prevented her tenfold return before she had even planted her Seed Money. She lacked gratitude; she never gave thanks for anything.

As John Hoshor writes: "The full figure of your return, however, is and must be important to you--important enough to call forth from you a fullhearted thankfulness as well as the necessary mental work.

Gratitude is the open door to Abundance. It helps to shorten the time required for your demonstration. Chemists tell us that for each ten degrees' increase in temperature, the speed of a chemical reaction doubles. So add the warmth of thankfulness, of gratitude, to your Seed Money formula--all along the line."

Gratitude is an indispensable catalyst in the working of the Law of Tenfold Return.

I asked the young lady if she knew of the custom of saying Grace before meals.

She replied that she did.

"In saying Grace," I told her, "you are giving thanks to God before the object of the thanks has been received--and as if it had already been received."

The sowing of Seed Money and the reaping of its harvest of multiplied return is exactly the same. Before we can expect more, we must give thanks for that which we already have.

Everything is in its Source, from God, what we have already received and what we are receiving [at present through the Law of Tenfold Return] as well as what we are going to receive in the future by the promise of Grace; for "of Him and through Him and to Him are all things" [Rom 11:36].

By giving thanks for what we already have--including that part which we are giving as Seed Money--we assist in expanding our Seed Money to its full tenfold return.

Dr. Ervin Seale of the Church of the Truth, New York, says: "Expansion is the law of life." And Gratitude an absolutely necessary part of expressing the value and direction that Life is taking.

[Gratitude is the energy-polarity that serves as a magnet to attract our tenfold return to us--physically.]

When the young lady learned of this--and consciously expressed gratitude in every area of her life of which she was consciously aware—she began to see results from working the Law of Tenfold Return.

So many people--not yet understanding that as God is Substance, so God is also the Source of the Tenfold Return--they omitted God in their attempts to practice Seed Money. They have not been keeping their eye upon the doughnut; but upon the hole.

God is Infinite everything, not limited nothingness. These truths have seemed to create a paradox for some, who rationalize that a specific Tenfold Return is nothing but a limitation. This is not the case.

As SEED MONEY says: "You may be told by someone that laying claim to a specific amount limits you. This is not the Law. Claiming a specific amount makes the demonstration both easier and more rapid. Actually, you do not limit yourself by making a claim for a specific amount because you can apply and reapply the principle an endless number of times either in succession or concurrently."

A practitioner worked the Principle of Seed Money and invariably received her Tenfold Return on Seed Money she had sown both in succession and concurrently. She could conceive of each gift's tenfold return without nterference with the return on other gifts. Most people, however, find it easier to practice the Law of Tenfold Return in succession.

Because of subtle negative thoughts which seem to originate with many people when they have "many irons in the fire," it is recommended that they, at first, sow their Seed Money in succession. Then each tenfold return helps to fortify faith in the next.

One of the doubts that may arrive especially in concurrent Seed Money harvesting is that regarding Source. This doubt also arises in single Seed Money demonstrations when the individual does not have firmly fixed in his consciousness that God is the Source of his Supply and that the words of Jesus, "Father, I thank thee that thou has heard me. And I knew that thou hearest me always" [Joh 11:41, 42] are as equally true today as they were in Palestine nearly two thousand years ago.

As John Hoshor said: "Do not pay the slightest attention to WHERE your return is coming from. That is neither your work nor your responsibility. The Infinite--God--takes care of both the means and the manner. Your work is to claim the tenfold return of your gift and to leave all constructive ways open for it to reach you.

"Seed Money return is EXPECTED money return. The means by which it comes to you and the manner in which it comes to you may be unexpected—more than likely it will be unexpected--but the return itself is EXPECTED."

Because the way and manner of your tenfold return is generally unexpected, some people do not recognize their tenfold return, even when they have received it.

A part-time typist worked one day a week for a leading metropolitan newspaper. Her workday at the paper was Friday. One Friday she received from a friend a copy of SEED MONEY. That Sunday she made a special Seed Money donation to her church.

On the next Thursday she told the man in the newspaper office who had given her the booklet: "Seed Money doesn't work. I still haven't received my return--although I believed 100%."

He questioned her: "But why are you working today--and also yesterday--when your only workday here is on Fridays?"

"Oh," she replied. "I'm replacing a regular typist who went away on a short trip."

"Let me call the personnel office and see why you were picked for the extra work," the man said, who had given her the SEED MONEY booklet. Five minutes later he told the temporary typist: "Personnel said there was no special reason for giving you the extra assignment--when the girl opened the page to the list of their qualified parttime typists her finger just fell by your name."

The typist's face suddenly glowed: "Oh, I did get my Tenfold Return after all. It is returned to me through the two unexpected extra days of work here--doing what I most enjoy doing."

She had received her tenfold return before she had given up. Some people always give up before they get their return because they set a time limitation when they plant their Seed Money. That is a great mistake.

A long time ago a Latin American public official kept me waiting for several hours after the appointment was due. When he finally arrived I said rather crossly: "Aren't any of you Latin Americans ever on time?"

He replied, smilingly, "No, but we don't have ulcers."

Ulcers, as medical science shows, are caused by worry, and time limitations which we ourselves set and give power to create most worries. Worry about man's measurement called time can be halted by the realization that God knows but one unit of time--NOW. It is said that "tomorrow never comes." This is perfectly true, for when tomorrow is here it is no longer tomorrow--but today.

A woman who owned a gift shop repeatedly planted Seed Money and repeatedly failed to receive her tenfold return. She couldn't understand it for, she said: "I know that the Principle of Seed Money works. Why doesn't it work for me?"

We analyzed her problem. She always said: I have received X dollars (tenfold the expect sum given) in return, with good to all concerned. Thank you. Thank you. Thank you."

After talking it out, we found that she always [in the back of her mind] added a fuure date for her return--whether for one day or one week later--which negated her statement that she had received the return.

I told her that we find the Promise in the Book of the prophet Isaiah, "And it shall come to pass, that before they call, I will answer; and while they are yet speaking, I will hear" [Isaiah 65:24].

When we give our Seed Money and claim our return we must KNOW that our tenfold return has ALREADY been made. Any thoughts that the return will only be made in the future will postpone our return indefinitely.

The gift shop owner saw her error--dissolved all thoughts of time limitation and thanked God for her return NOW. And then she began working the Principle of Seed Money successfully.

SEED MONEY answers the question, "How long will it take?--"There is no time in the Infinite. Time is a human concept. Do your work faithfully and go happily about your normal business. As certainly as the day will dawn on the morrow your effort will be rewarded."

John Hoshor wrote: "There is an after-the-fact technique that invariably helps shorten the time required for the Law's demonstration. It aids in registering the pattern clearly in your consciousness.

"Imagine that you have the return in hand. That much you must do. Then, to that add the mental picture of exactly what you are going to do with the return. If you intend to spend it, see yourself obtaining exactly what you want and using it. Go through the details of whatever is its function several times.

Or, it may be that you are going to put the Seed Money return to yet another investment. Carry out the investment in your mind. ... Or, imagine yourself sending a check to your church or to a favorite social service organization as the next SEED MONEY step in establishing stability."

I know a businessman who could not succeed at the Law of Tenfold Return because of his mental attitude of lack. As I explained to him:

"A good gardener does not only cultivate flowers--he cultivates SOIL. Thoughts which you are always sending out compose the soil of your life. If you are constantly projecting thoughts of lack you will have barren soil. If you project thoughts of plenty your soil will be rich in the humus of Sufficiency, and it is that soil in which your Seed Money grows."

Jesus tells us that in the parable of the sower: "Behold, a sower went forth to show:

And when he sowed, some seeds fell by the wayside, and the birds came and devoured them up; some fell upon stony places where they had not much earth; and forthwith they sprung up because they had no deepness of earth; but when the sun was up they were scorched; and because they had no root, they withered away.

And some fell among thorns; and the thorns sprung up, and choked them; but other fell onto good ground, and brought forth fruit, some an hundredfold, some sixty-fold, some thirty-fold" [Matt 13:3-8].

The businessman said, "True, but how can I prepare my soil?"

And I quoted: "All [thought] is an action of the conscious on the subconscious. Money is God's idea of circulation. This idea I now accept as the basis of all my financial affairs. Money is God's activity, that it does good when it serves need. I use it with wisdom; I release it with joy; I send it forth without fear for I know that under Divine Law it comes back to me" [quote from Dr. Ray C. Barker, in "Money is God In Action."].

The businessman put these ideas into practice and was soon able to reap abundant harvests from his Seed Money, as the others had.

It is very important for us all to get out of our mental patterns of poverty, to realize that, as God knows no lack, neither do we.

John Hoshor writes: "The Law is there for you to use just as air is there for you to breathe. Would you choose to spend your life without fresh air? In an oxygen-deprived, smoke-filled room or in an area constantly saturated with smog? Such conditions take their toll in life and health for those who choose them or who permit themselves to live in such surroundings. Similarly, those who are ignorant of the Law of Seed Money and how it works suffer with unfulfilled needs, from the lack of many of the desirable experiences of life which in our day require money to purchase.

"The cost of living, at or near a record high, continues to mount. Rents, mortagages and taxes are the highest ever and are still increasing. Food has never been costlier, nor of poor quality in general. Today all children must be college-educated to compete in their generation successfully. Wage and salary increases do not solve this problem. Other and greater Sources of income, trade, barter and exchange are needed.

"The saying that the rich get richer has never been truer. Or that the poor get poorer. The reasons for both are fundamental. "Gummint" favors the rich, who daily apply the Law although may not be aware of it. This is why Jesus spoke to the Rich and instructed them to give away their money. They have a surplus above their living needs that makes it unnecessary to pay any more than casual attention to those needs. So they do not multiply NEEDS in their consciousness--not theirs nor anyone else's. They live surrounded by riches and the evidence of riches.

"Blessed are the poor in spirit because they will be filled," makes no sense to the rich. The Law always works. The direction in which it works depends solely upon the contents of an individual's consciousness. Multiplying needs, one is poor. Multiplying from one Source and giving away the excess, one remains conscious of need and is able to assist those overwhelmed by need. But multiplying riches alone merely leaves an individual insensate; so use the Law of Ten with discretion and not with obsessions around obtaining and acquiring, for the purpose of hoarding.

The poor are constantly thinking and talking about their needs. Yet, the Universal Law of Life is that upon which ou focus your attention--THAT is what you attract into your life and experience.

"The individual's only relief from poverty is to get himself out of the vicious cycle of thinking of need and poverty and stop focusing on these, and instead focus on sharing, giving and being willing to receive.

One woman said, "I can never even start to practice Seed Money because I can't even plant any--I never have enough money to spare. I'm too far behind."

I advised her to open her Bible to Proverbs, Chapter 11 and then read verse 24. She read: "There exists the one that is scattering and yet is being increased; also the one that is keeping back from what is right, but it results only in want."

In other words, there are those who circulate that which they have, and what they have increases; and there are those who hold fast to every penny they have, and they reduce their own options.

This verse from scripture changed her way of thinking. It made her realize WHY she had been unable to increase what she had. She has become an ardent follower of the Law of Tenfold Return.

John Hoshor gave another example of how he helped someone to thrive through the principle of Seed Money:

"A man I know by the name of Sheldon found a way out. This man had many ups and downs. He was twice a millionaire, both times when a million dollars was a lot of money. Some months ago Sheldon's business failed. The immediate cause was a bad credit loss. Yet he knew there was a deeper cause.

"I suggested to Sheldon the John D. Rockefeller technique of giving. When he answered that he had given not thousands, but hundreds of thousands, of dollars away I knew that he spoke the Truth. Sheldon has never been known to refuse a request for help. I explained to him that although giving was necessary, just giving was not enough, that one can easily go bankrupt giving without return.

"He listened for an hour as I outlined the principles involved in Seed Money to him.

"Sheldon asked, 'With what do I start? I'm flat broke.' He had $3 in his pocket. On my advice he exchanged his $3 for 300 new pennies and started giving them out one at a time. I received the first one. Each time he gave a penny he would multiply it in his consciousness and see the multiplied return as having been made to him. The same evening, before he had given out all of his pennies, a long forgotten creditor came to his home and paid him $12 on an old bill.

"On my advice Sheldon went again to the bank and this time brought back 200 new nickels. Again he started giving them away, one at a time, each time following the Seed Money technique. Within three days he was called in as consultant on a marketing problem and received $250 for a half day's work.

"Still working the Seed Money formula, this time he began with $100 worth of new quarters. While he was busy giving these out and multiplying and claiming his return, two friends contacted him and offered to finance him in a new business venture. All the capital he needed was placed at his disposal.

"Sheldon came to my apartment and we talked over the situation.

"He said, 'Although I have been in business in New York City for forty years, actually, like Moses, I have been wandering in the wilderness. Never before have I known what I was doing.'

He insisted that he would not have any more 'downs' in his life because he had learned the Seed Money formula and practiced it; and it worked. He still gives but now he multiplies and claims his tenfold return, and his new business is prospering mightily."

We have seen that just giving is not enough to work the Law of Tenfold Return, but "Why is giving necessary?"

John Hoshor says, "The farmer who wants a crop must give to the earth--must sow or plant the seed--otherwise he will harvest only the weeds that happen to grow. . . . When you were born the first thing the doctor did was to hold you up by the heels and smack your little bottom. You gave out with a squawk and that started your breathing. Breathing itself is both a giving and a receiving. So is your very life; for discontinue either exhaling or inhaling and your life is over.

"When you want the lights on you flick the switch that opens the circuit and begins the flow of current. The entire Universe is a series of energy circuits--from the earth and other planets in their orbits to the particles of the atom in their orbits. Shut off the flow anywhere along the line and the result is emptyness."

In James Stephens classic, "The Crock of Gold," he observes, "You must be fit to give before you can be fit to receive. The plain and simple truth is that you must start giving before you can start receiving. This is the kind of Universe in which we live."

A secretary couldn't understand why prayer alone without giving Seed Money, wouldn't work. I told her that Prayer with Thanksgiving are complementary essentials, for "in every thing by prayer and supplication with thanksgiving let your request be made known unto God" [Philippians 4:6]. The gift itself not only subconsciously sets in motion a cycle of ever-increasing energy (which returns to you in your tenfold return) but it also serves to fix firmly in your mind the image of the desired return.

The story of the great prophet Eliyah and the widow of Zarephath, where the widow's scant food supply multiplied so that she and the Prophet Elijah, "and her house did eat many days" [1 Kings 17:10-16] proves this truth.

` As Dr. Henry M. Ellis writes, "As Elijah proved, an act of faith, evidenced by giving, is prerequisite to receiving."

The importance of the doing--of actually giving--is shown not only in the Old and New Testaments, but in other religiouis works through the ages.

Omitting the actual sowing of Seed Money in the Law of Tenfold Return is the same as sewing without thread--you make a lot of motions, but you don't get anywhere.

The secretary accepted this, and with some further help was able to practice of the Law of Tenfold Return. She was more fortunate than a man who, receiving a SEED MONEY booklet, complained that he had not a penny to his name--he had spent his laqst fifteen cents on a biscuit.

I turned his booklet to the page in SEED MONEY where it says, "How can I give when I don't have any money? Then you must start with your muscles, with labor and the sweat of thy brow until you have received some of the currency of the realm. Then start giving it and claiming the multiplication of the tenfold return back to yourself. Continue this as you continue breathing and soon you will be prosperous and surrounded by Sufficiency."

Actually, no one ever achieved security working either at labor or at a white collar job. Those who experience Freedom are those who organize their minds for self-sufficiency, who direct employees on the one hand and who direct their multiplied clains to the Infinite on the other. As a matter of fact, you do not need to hire anyone to become rich-in-freedom, provided you know the Seed Money technique and use it patiently and persistently. Likewise, you can be an employee, and by using the Seed Money formula constantly in your life you can become more self-reliant than your employer if he were to fail to use the formula himself.

In truth, when people only want money and the power that derives from money, you know and I know, they get handed over to Satan and all sorts of temptations, to learn how to place limits on their appetites. So, let's not use the word "Rich" as a goal or objective because that word implies excess. Let's plan to get off the train at the stop called "Self-Sufficiency."

The "down-and-out" man asked, "Who would hire me?" And I said, "We have some packages to take to the Post Office right now. You can Seed Money your labor and I will give you ten dollars besides."

He cried out, "What? Manual labor? Me? Never." And he ran from the office leaving his SEED MONEY booklet behind. I tried to catch him; but he had gotten into the elevator before I was able to do so.

This man had counted himself "down-and-out." He will not get up off the canvas until he realizes that the Law of Tenfold Return decrees that ten times something is that something multiplied by ten. Ten times nothing, however, is still nothing.

An engineer understood this perfectly. He saw that the Law of Tenfold Return was based upon a perfectly logical working of the Power of the Tithe and of Holy Law. But every time he planted Seed Money he began to wonder and speculate as to how and by what mechanics his return would come. So, it didn't come.

His problem was very simple. He did not exercise unquestioning faith, by merely permitting wonder but never doubting. He did not "let go and let God" determine the means to fulfill this Law.

SEED MONEY states: "Do you remember the saying, 'A little child shall lead them'? Why shall a little child lead them? Because it is easy for a child to imagine or wonder and because children practice imagination and wonder more than grown-ups do."

Jesus had said, "Yea; have ye never read, 'Out of the mouth of babes and sucklings thou hast perfected praise' [Matthew 21:16] ?

The engineer was advised to claim his expected return now, and leave the workings of his tenfold return to God. And he began to see that as a child can unquestioningly accept that good inevitably produces good, so can he unquestioningly see multiplication of his Seed Money in his life. Jesus had expressed this Truth, "For a good tree bringeth not forth corrupt fruit; neither doth a corrupt tree bring forth good fruit. For every tree is known by its own fruit. For of thorns men do not gather figs, nor of a bramble bush gather they grapes" [Luke 6:43-44].

Recognizing that the Law of Tenfold Return is part of the Universal One Law, the engineer applied to his practice of the Seed Money principle the same childlike faith required in all spiritual unfoldment, as Jesus said, "Whosoever shall not receive the kingdom of God as a little child, he shall not enter therein" [Mark 10:15].

The engineer's new success in demonstrating through the Law of Tenfold Return occurred because he now understood that it is a method originating with Jesus and the nation of Israel.

As John Hoshor wrote in SEED MONEY: "What is the formula that makes the Law of Seed Money work for you? . . . The formula is derived from Jesus. When properly used, it always produces the desired results." Jesus declared very openly: "What things soever ye desire, when ye pray, believe that ye receive them, and ye shall have them" {Mark 11:24]. And, that is exactly what He meant.

Quoting from SEED MONEY: "No words ever spoken or written in any language carry great or more far-reaching import than these words of the Great Master.

"Please note: You are not asked to join any organization. You are not asked to attend any meetings. You are not asked to subscribe to any dogma. You are not asked to follow any ritual. You are not asked to believe in any theories, opinions or suppositions. You are only asked to believe that you already have received whatever it is you want. Surely this is not too great a price for you to pay to achieve the self-sufficiency you want to have.

"Imagine that they are yours NOW. What could be easier? And it works. It works. IT WORKS. Anyone can prove it conclusively for themself.

`"To repeat, the ONLY THING you have to believe is that you have already receive that which you want. Your age does not matter. Your creed does not matter. Your race does not matter. Your familyi name does not matter. Your sex does not matter. Your political affiliation does not matter. Your nationality does not matter. Your education or lack of it does not matter.

"Simply believe that YOU HAVE ALREADY RECEIVED WHATEVER IT IS YOU NEED. No one else can limit you. If you want to limit yourself, though, you can. Otherwise the entire resources of the Universe may be yours to use (appropriately or inappropriately, your choice)."

One lady who had come to the United States from Eastern Europe wasn't having success with her practice of the Seed Money formula. She had a subconscious pattern of limitation due to an image of herself in her own mind that she, as a refugee, was a second-class citizen. She compounded the damage to herself by constantly dwelling on what she had lost instead of being in the HERE and NOW. She resented everyone who owned fine things such as she had lost.

With help, in time she came to realize that God knows only one class--FIRST CLASS--and that she as a child of God was the only person who could possibly even seem to demote her to poverty, in reality.

She came to see that she--not only in order to bring prosperity through the Law of Tenfold Return into her life but in order to attain peace of mind--had to obey the commandments as Jesus had stated them:

"And thou shalt love the Lord thy God with all thy heart, and with all thy soul, and with all thy mind, and with all thy strength: this is the first commandment. And the second is like namely this, Thou shalt love thy neighbour as thyself. There is none other commandment greater than these" [Mark 12:30-31].

Only then did this immigrant woman realize that she must lose her resentment against her neighbors if she was to take advantage of the Law of Tenfold Return.

By persistent meditation on these two greatest commandments and their place in her Life, she suddenly found herself able to make demonstrations occur which she, and she alone, had blocked for so long. She turned her once lonely life of self-punishment into a happy life of abundance and helpfulness to others. This helpfulness--a willingness and readiness to lend a helping hand--often provides opportunities to sow Seed Money under circumstances in which it is remarkably easy to visualize a return—Good for Good, multiplied tenfold.

John Hoshor related in SEED MONEY: "One morning not long ago I was waiting on a street corner in Manhattan for a bus to take me to my office. A man who had been sitting on a nearby bench arise and shuffled over to where I stood. We spoke and passed the time of day. I noticed that his clothes were old and torn and that instead of shoes he was wearing low-cut rubber overshoes. I asked the question which he had obviously expected me to ask.

"What happened to your shoes?"

"'Someone stole them while I was asleep last night,' he told me.

"'What are you going to do for shoes?'

"'That is what I have been wondering. I found these in the garbage back of the building where I slept,' he answered. He showed me the soles which were more holes than rubber.

"'What can you get a pair of shoes for?' I asked.

"'There's a shoe repair shop I know of where I can get an unclaimed repaired pair for $4 or maybe $5.'

"Then I asked him, 'Do you have the money?'

"'I don't have a cent,' he replied.

"'How near is the shoe repair shop?' I awked.

"He pointed, 'Only two blocks over that way.'

"'Let's walk over,' I suggested.

"When we reached the shoe repair shop I handed him $5. "'See what you can get with that. If you need more, tap on the window and I will come in.'

"In a few minutes he came out of the store wearing a comfortable looking pair of repaired shoes. He held out a dollar bill towards me, saying, 'I got these for four bucks.'

"'Keep the dollar,' I told him.

"We walked together to the corner and shook hands, thanking each other.

"He asked, 'Why do you thank me?'

"'Because I am happy that I was able to be of service to you,' I told him.

"We wished each other good luck and I went on my way back to the bus stop.

"As I walked I silently repeated over the Seed Money formula, 'I have received $50 in return, with good to all concerned. Thank you.' When I arrived at my office, business took over and I forgot the incident completely.

"Mind you, please, I have practiced the formula for years. I have worked it almost countless times, both on a small scale and on a large scale. I have seen friends make it work many times. So, not only did I believe I had received the $50 in return, I KNEW.

"That night as I opened the door of the apartment house in which I live, a pretty girl came out and smilingly thanked me. I noticed she carried a musical score from 'The Pajama Game,' and I asked her,

"'Are you a singer?'

"'No,' she answered, 'I'm a receptionist at a call center service , but I'm taking singing lessons.'

"Who is your teacher?' I asked.

"She mentioned the name of a voice teacher who had been a friend of mine for many years but whom I had not seen for fifteen years. I told her my name and asked her to remember me to her teacher. She said that she would and went on her way.

"I went to my apartment, showered and put on fresh clothes. As I was starting out to keep an appointment, the manager of the apartment house came to my door and told me I had a call over her phone. I answered it. The voice teacher was calling and asked me to come to his studio. I went at 10:30 that evening. After we had shaken hands and congratulated each other on none of the fifteen years showing, he said,

"'John, before you moved to California you did some publicity for me which proved very profitable to me. You never sent me a bill.'

"I explained that I had done it as a favor, that it had not required any time, merely a phone call.

"He said, 'Had you billed me then, I could not have paid you, but I would like to pay you now.'

"He walked over to the Baby Grand piano and picked up a check already made out and offered it to me saying,

"'Will $50 be all right?'

"I answered him, '$50 is exactly right.'

"There may be some who will scoff and say that I have linked two events which had no fundamental relationship to each other. However, the wiser will believe me when I say that the $5 given to the needy man for shoes and the $50 out of the blue for a forgotten service were as surely linked to each other as my fingers are linked to my hands.

"Here was a penniless, needy man in rags, without shoes who unknowingly brought to me $45 in profit in added self-sufficiency, which it is conceivable, might never have otherwise reached me. How was this possible? It was possibly only because I knew the Principle of Seed Money, the Law of Tenfold Return, and I took the opportunity that came my way to aid a fellow human being and of then applying the Law and claiming my multiplied return. I thanked him sincerely before we parted and should he ever read this, I would thank him again."

A unique way of sowing Seed Money was that of the advertising manager of a magazine. He read a copy of SEED MONEY and said that he wanted to Seed Money space in his magazine to advertise that booklet.

He did. For nearly a year his advertising revenue increased substantially, which he credits to his practice of Seed Money.

The practice of Seed Money from generation to generation can produce self-sufficiency hardly conceivable to the average person. When one sees a work of art, hears beautiful music, receives the most effective healing assistance from real healers or witnesses advances in space technology, they may not know that many achievements in these fields would not have been possible without the practice of Seed Money by the Guggenheim family.

From 1847 when Meyer Guggenheim immigrated to America until today, a fortune that has conservatively been estimated at $200,000,000 ($20 billion in 2000 dollars) has circulated and increased for but one purpose, as Ambassador Harry Guggenheim says, "for the progress of man."

Benefits the great Guggenheim fortune have given mankind—through financing, building and developing ideas--are inestimable, and the selection of the title of the Guggenheim family biography bears witness to its growth: SEED MONEY.

The thinking of the Guggenheim family has been the very opposite of lack. The word "can't" doesn't seem to be in their vocabulary. And the ability to know that success is right here, even before it has been visibly manifest, has not only characterized Guggenheim success, but is an indispensable factor in practicing Seed Money itself.

As John Hoshor says, "So that there can be no vagueness or misunderstanding in the mind of any reader as to how anyone makes his claim on the Infinite for the multiplied return of his gift, I wish to point out that he does so by believing he has already received such multiplied return. It is as simple as that.

"Instead of continually saying as many do, 'I want,' 'I need,' or 'I do not have,' SAY 'I have' and 'it's coming, I know.'

"In addition to making the gifr to start the flow of prosperity to you--believing that you have ALREADY RECEIVED your multiplied return is your only work.

As it says in SEED MONEY, "There is no telling how the return which you claim will come to you. The only telling for certain is that it will come. You do not want some loved one to die and will you the amount you claim. You do not want to receive it as a result of an injury to yourself. So always include in your multiplied Seed Money claim--or for that matter whenever you draw upon the Infinite for anything, the provision "with good to all concerned." In this manner you protect yourself and others who may be concerned.

"Carefully check your motive in each of your Seed Money operations to make certain that there is no content of harm, or intended harm, in it towards anyone concerned. Whether the money is primarily for yourself, or for others, or simply for reserve to practice proving the Law, it should manifest with equal ease.

The Law does not care. But if there is harm in your consciousness towards anyone, that harm will multiply also and return to fall upon your own head. You cannot fool--nor sidestep--the Law."

This is equally true in regard to your physical health as well as your financial health, for God is the Source of all Good and "no good thing will be withheld from them that walk uprightly" [Psalms 84:11].

Expecting to be healed from any ailment is the first step toward physical healing. And in the practice of hygiene and nutrition--just as in the practice of the Tenfold Return--what you give to your body comes back to you ten times--as feeling good or as feeling worse. The spirit in which you give [to yourself as well as to others] is the most important thing about your gifts or your health practices: you WILL reap what you sow.

"When an opportunity to give a gift [to someone in need] or to nurture your body [with wholesome food and not food cravings], if you consider it but then decide against it, you are saying in effect, "I better not; I may [something else] myself." And so, as you say, you will need—most certainly--something ELSE yourself.

"If you give grudgingly or with calculations in mind, these configurations that you imagine will return upon you, ten times, also.

"If, however, you give boldly, generously, full-heartedly, impulsively, it shall be returned to you tenfold in the same manner." What is important is that "in due season we shall reap, if we faint not" [Galatians 6:9].

This is explained very clearly in the Bible: "He which soweth sparingly shall reap also sparingly; and he which soweth bountifully shall reap also bountifully. Every man according as he purposeth in his heart, so let him give; not grudgingly, or of necessity: for God loveth a cheerful giver" [II Corinthians 9:6-7].

Never pass by an opportunity to sow Seed Money. A lost opportunity to give is a lost opportunity to receive.

John Joshor illustrates this in an incident which happened to him: "The fastest and in some ways most interesting return on a SEED MONEY tenfold claim that I know of happened to me quite recently.

"I was on my way to a branch post office with an armload of parcel post packages. In addition, I carried--unwrapped but in its own display case—a small appliance I was then distributing. I intended to deliver it to a local purchaser on my way back.

"As I hurried up the crowded street I passed a blind man with a cup. I thought to myself, 'I'd give him something if I weren't loaded down.'

"Almost instantly I recognized the negative application of the Law. I turned and struggled back through the crowd, reaching the blind man and asked him to stop for a second.

"I laid my packages on the sidewalk, took all the change from my pocket and put it in his cup. It made a good noise and it seemed as if he were almost on the verge of opening his eyes to LOOK. However, he did not, but repeated his thanks. I recovered my packages, reached the post office and mailed them. Then, taking my unwrapped appliance, I turned to leave the post office. A man stopped me saying,

"'I'm interested in that product. May I see it?'

"'Certainly,' I answered.

"We stopped at the first writing counter near the entrance and I took the appliance out of its box and showed him how it worked. It happened to operate on batteries and their sound attracted a small crowd. The man who had inquired looked at it, then handed me his card, saying,

"'Where can I buy a couple hundred of these things?'

"'I distribute them,' I told him. 'I'll be happy to supply you.'

"He said, 'First, let me buy the special delivery stamp I came for, then we'll do some business.'

"On the way to my office he introduced himself. He was an Ohio distributor for one of the reducing food companies and he was in New York looking for a product he could use as a premium to open accounts with dealers. He bought 200, did not ask for the discount to which he was entitled and which I gave him. He paid cash. I do not know exactly how much I gave the blind man. I had made my claim for a general tenfold return, and I'm quite certain that the profit from that sale represented a full measure return, running over.

"Perhaps the most significant part of the transaction was that the buyer was a happy with his purchase as a child is with a shining new toy." Here was

John Hoshor himself getting back a tenfold return in according with the Law of Seed Money.

The Law of Seed Money is in itself very simple: In giving money to your church or school or to anyone you know who has a real and legitimate "need," or in any other way using money to bless someone, help someone do something they could never do of their own accord, aid someone at a distance whom you don't know but whose testimony moves you, you have not only the right and the privilege but you have also the duty of claiming--from the Infinite—a tenfold return, in money or in kind. To claim it is to have received it already subjectively. In a short time, it will also come to you physically.

The Law of Seed Money is the KEY to using the Infinite substance of God: "Now he that ministereth seed to the sower both minister bread for your food and multiply your seed down, and increase the fruits of your righteousness" [II Corinthians 9:10].

The Law of Seed Money works in accord with the words of Jesus: "All things, whatsoever ye shall ask in prayer, believing, ye shall receive" [Matthew 21:22].

The formula for practicing Seed Money is merely a way to help you prove these words in your own experience. Remember, the formula is very simple:

1. Plant seed money. Give the amount you wish to the person you want to assist in some way.

2. Immediately upon making your gift, cultivate a claim and as soon as you are alone, focus on your tenfold claim on the Infinite in a way that expresses

something like this: 'My return on helping "X" is $... so that there would be good out of that gift for all concerned. Thank you.'

3. Make sure you believe in your claim. If you need to rehearsed it a few times in your mind until it rings "reasonable" to you, do that, especially just before you fall asleep. Confirm that claim whenever the thought comes up, but don't make an obsession out of it. It is not necessary to overwork it.

4. Begin your gifts at a very modest level, sufficient that your gift and your multiplied return are significant enough, you will do the mental work to retrieve your return. If you begin at so high a value that you wonder from where the money will return, you have defeated yourself. Avoid doubts, or they will manifest as Nothing.

5. Never tell anyone of your claim or of your manner of manifesting. Do this in private, whether silently, aloud or written down as a note to yourself. The only person you have to impress is your own consciousness with the reasonableness of your claim.

6. In the event that your claim does not return the correct amount to you, or does not return as repidly as you believe it should, thank God for the lesson of learning how to be sufficient in poverty, and mull over the thought how you will make yourself available to help another, in the near future, fully faithful to continue the process. Simply assume you erred somehow, and move on.

7. Affirm your willingness to keep up the practice of Generosity insofar as you are able. And then, no matter how small the amount is, when someone expects a TIP, tip generously. When someone asks for alms, give your lunch money. When someone on the bus needs carfare, give it to them. When your coworker goes without eating for lack of money, share with them. And your generosity will begin to return good to you if you give gifts in the spirit of complete Trust in the Infinite's generosity toward yourself.

Scientists have explored the Universe with powerful telescopes and with powerful microscopes. In all of their search and research they have found only one thing. From the farthest star to the most infinitesimal part of the atom the only thing scientists have been able to find is energy.

Energy fills the Universe; the Universe IS energy; the Infinite is energy. Then it should come as no surprise that there is a fluid, plastic, invisible energy that flows evermore through the mind, to the senses. It is an unlimited energy, and it will flow into whatever pattern you conceive of—good or ill. This is why thinking--only--of what is beneficial and harmless and progressive is essential for joyful life. And inasmuch as all energy works in a circuit, the energy flowing through your mind brings back to you precisely what you send out in your thoughts, words and emotions. It all comes back upon you.

If you pattern Infinite energy flowing through your mind with Lacking, debts and needs, Lacking is the experience you get back. And if you pattern your energies with the desire to be useful and of service, what will return to you is a God-given role or place of great interest and productivity. But if you program your thoughts and expectations with failures and despair, that will return to you also. [This is WHY drugs are so harmful; they promote the visualization of suffering].

Each of us is the Director, the Selector, the Chooser, the Decider--which of the thoughts that run through our mind are the thoughts we want to express and manifest. That option is called "Free Will." Bugs and animals don't have Free Will; they don't have options from which to choose.

The Law of Tenfold Return is the Law of Loaves and Fishes. For the necessary material things of life, we must give in order to get back what is sufficient to live--"for your heavenly Father knoweth that ye have need of all these things"--and the principle of Seed Money shall help you stand on your own two feet, despite and no matter what circumstances may influence society, culture or experience.

No words or thoughts or emotions of ours ever return to us unfilled. Therefore, be always exceedingly careful that all words from the mouth and thoughts and emotions are positive and beneficial, constructive and specifically applied to doing good.

By guiding and directing that Infinite energy forever flowing through the mind by words and thoughts and emotions that are beneficial, we bless fellow human beings with gifts in appropriate promptings, high expectations, due praise and the push to clarity of thought and Truth itself. The return in giving out God's Truth is that ten times more truth returns as wisdom and clarity.

And so it is. Amen.

SELF-FINANCING A NEW COMMUNITY WHEN MONEY IS SCARCE

STEP 1. Establish Promise agree ments for labor and begin sharing love with each other, referred to previously.

STEP 2. LEGAL MANDATES Collateral and Group Organization--Once you have a group doing favors for each other, what happens is that somebody needs money, and nobody has enough money to make a commitment.

What you're going to do next is set up Community Entity (a Role or Job that can rotate) whose Mission is to establish the Credit Rating of the Group, to further the purposes of the Neighborhood, whether that becomes :

* Purchasing Together,

* Maintaining Common Grounds,

* Managing some Business ventures together. Naturally, we begin with the assumption that Nobody has much cash. But as any pawn broker will tell you, the things that people possess comprise Collateral that can be held as security for Loans. This is to say that, people in the community willing to allow their Objects of Value to be held or sold as COLLATERAL for the whole Community, then become Recipients of loans which the Community is able to secure in its

Name--

IF NOT from banks at this time, at least at favorable rates from local pawn brokers.

Not only does the Neighborhood now have an opportunity to swap Promises and Favors, everybody can now Empty Themselves of all their Excess Stuff so it becomes the very Collateral from which a membership finances all its Ventures, both Individual loans and Group Projects.

EXAMPLES.--Stamp collections and collections of all kinds. Jewelry that nobody wears. Extra cars and car parts; extra tools; guns; old cameras, bric a brac, boat anchors and white elephants.

The person in charge of collateral must have an archetypal personality that one would call a manager, a promoter, a wheeler-dealer with impeccable honesty.

ASSESSING COLLATERAL

All collateral should be retained that is small and can be liquidated quickly, or if large and ungainly, it should be traded for something that IS SMALL and CAN be liquidated quickly and easily. To keep the Manager honest, the deal they get is this:

* Whatever they sell they put the money in the

Community Account Box.

* If the Manager steals money, then Everybody loses their money.

* If the Manager is honest and all Collateral can be accounted for; then after four years, the Manager retires that position and the Community builds him or her a new home in the Community.

* If it is found after the Manager leaves that something is actually missing, then the new House itself becomes collateral for the Community, and the dishonest Manager must leave.

SECURING MONEY AND VALUABLES

Anything which people lawfully obtain can be brought to the Manager for scrutiny as potential Collateral for future Credit. What actually tends to happen is that the person deemed Manager teaches everyone in the Neighborhood, very quickly, what comprises good Collateral and what doesn't.

The outcome of that is, when someone in the Community acquires an inheritance, a gift they're not really thrilled with, or make a super trade that they can't utilize themselves, guess where they go?

Thus, you can see this Position generates a great deal of focused Value in the Community.

Where can money and valuables be kept?

Bank safety deposit boxes are no longer safe; they are accessible by others, at will. Thus, all small items (rings, gold or silver coins, estate jewelry, stock portfolios, deeds, lines of credit) must be inventoried, assayed, labeled and hidden.

What is true is that, if you look at the level of debt associated with Banking these days, and the practice of utilizing gasoline and oil revenues as the Main prop for American currency, it's probably not a good idea to depend on the FDIC to protect your money, in any case. The small amount of interest that is generated is not worth the risk of losing everything. So, just keep utilizing your local Pawn Broker for loans until Banks turn over a new honest leaf; and don't hold your breath until that occurs.

Your group may want to quickly set up your own Pawn Shop or Credit Union; so, now your neighborhood needs to think about organizing itself to conduct business on behalf of its Neighbors.

For that step, you will need an attorney who can discuss with the members of your Group the kinds of legal organizations which might be suitable for you. Arriving at such a decision is beyond the scope of this monograph.

However, just remember a 501(c)(3) organization is expected to keep detailed books, that a professional accountant must be engaged.

Swapping clubs--books, tools, furnishings.

The simple fact is, once you start making and keeping Promises with your friends, you will discover what they have and what they lack. It just comes naturally. So, what makes sense for the Next Step in Community Building is to Organize what the Group HAS IN EXCESS OVER true NEEDS.

This also serves the purpose of making sure Everyone else has ACCESS to Essentials, under the Promise System.

EXAMPLES ~*~ Let's say I'm an auto mechanic, and I have most of the tools I need most of the time. You are a single lady, and you don't know a box-end wrench from an adjustable one. And John over here sells widgets, and happens to have 16 cases of screwdrivers that he found in his garage.

HOW DO YOU ORGANIZE THIS, TO BENEFIT EVERYBODY?

Simple. Make a list and pass it around. ESSENTIAL TOOLS that you can't lend out don't need to be written down; ESSENTIAL tools that can be loaned On A Promise and EXTRA tools that can be given away freely or stocked in a Tool Library.

Once the Community Tools List is made up, everybody knows what is Present and what is Lacking. It's Good to do a new Inventory each year, preferably in Autumn. This is because Men like to receive Tools as wintertime Gifts from their Women.

This same Technique can be utilized for Books, Garden Equipment, Storage Equipment, Children's Books and Whole Toys, Community Kitchen Equipment, Household items, as well as for accumulating Surplus Items for Refurbishing and Sale at a Gathering later on.

WHAT ADVANTAGES ACCRUE?

What occurs in Suburbia is that Each Person must pay to set up an entire workshop, who does any hand- or craft work must occupy a house large enough to STORE it all, must keep track of it ALL. This is a waste of family resources.

Rather, if all Essential Tools are in fact available for checking out, FREE, as needed from a neighborhood Source, the natural outcome of Group resource planning is that everyone doesn't need to buy Everything.

The costs of Community Resource Planning are two: Secure Space for Stuff and Supervision during "Business" Hours. Secure Space means someone's garage or tool shed with a lock on it. Supervision during business hours means the supervisor should have an independent source of income so s/he can hang around most of the time, keep order and keep track.

In the process of securing neighborhood tools, what happens is that space is created to handle other neighborhood functions.

Buying cooperatives--food, fuel, fabrics.

One of the best-kept secrets of modern marketing is that Buying In Lots Is Cheap. What Stores try to do is to second-guess people's Wants, and Charge For It.

Now that your Group has a place to store tools, equipment and books, it's a simple, natural step to begin group purchase of essential staples.

The fact is: Every human needs the SAME ESSENTIALS.

Let's list what Human Essentials consist of:

* Clean air--Forest and Land Management

* Clean water--Drain-off management

* Waste Management--Recycling, Refurbishing

* Infectious Disease Management -- Sanitation

* Seasonal Crops--grains, nuts, produce, fruits

* Continuous Fragile Staples--milk, soy products, bread, greens, sprouts

* Yarns, threads, Fabrics and notions; or manufactured clothing shoes seconds'.

* Wood and all its By-products: paper, chips, logs, planks boards

* Stone for permanent structures, drain-off, road-building, and septic systems; GLASS

* COST *

What is TRUE is that everything on this list can be had for labor costs only where Land is available.

Yes, Life is practically Free where people have land.

However, EVEN BEFORE the People have Land FREE AND CLEAR, they can do a lot to Free Themselves from the DEMANDS of Money:

* Layers and layers of registrations

* Commuting and all its costs

* Layers and layers of taxation,

* Obtaining as a pleasure-substitute for companionship,

* Obsessing over collecting things and caring

for it all, and neglect of human essentials, namely, Rest and Fun.

When people purchase in lots and from original sources, cost is minimal. To benefit from rock-bottom prices, Everyone gives time and a little effort. And then Just a little bit of money goes a long, long way.

Let's say you are part of a neighborhood that has space for its tools and garden implements, and you want to move on towards Community Buying. How do you do that?

The same way Retailers do. Shop price and bulk. Buy from growers and use your time to organize, package, and distribute small amounts to neighbors. *Food co-ops can also* buy and distribute lots of wood, meat, 'remainders' of consumer items including clothes, shoes, and notions, if they keep to Simple sources.

One full-time person can organize a whole operation and save the Community 80% of its food bill; liberate everyone from half their shopping trips; and provide a venue for camaraderie, sharing, and common ground good times that nobody had time for before.

Buying as a Group FREES EVERYBODY to hang out together and spend time GIVING AWAY what they want to Get Back.

If the people decide to keep their savings, they

can choose whether to spend money on themselves or GIVE THAT AWAY too.

PROGRESS CHECK

Okay, to summarize how far we've come. We have a group of people who decided to start making and keeping Promises to each other. So they start DOING THINGS for each other that they had never done before. And the outcome is that they begin to love each other.

So, then they POOL their tools, books, and equipment so they only have to buy what nobody already has stored in the Equipment Room.

So then they start buying commodities and building materials in common so they don't need to make as much money, and they can have more time to play together. They begin to spend even more of their time giving each other Essentials.

What they can now expect (REMEMBER--SEED MONEY?) is to get back TEN times what they are giving away. Folks are merely giving Gifts back and forth between THEMSELVES. THIS IS THE FORMULA for manifesting FREE ABUNDANCE. Study it. Put it into Practice.

A Skills Bank for Neighboring and Labor Sharing

Now that you have freed up some capital from

mere survival, it's time to think about the Options which that opens up for you. Naturally, some of you will jump off at this point, because there will be special agendas you want to follow.

This is good, because you are now a self-sustaining Community. But, for those of you who want to PRESS ON to a level of diversity and education not heretofore achieved, the way to proceed is clear before you.

Up til now, you have only utilized one person full-time, and the rest of the people have only worked cooperatively as Volunteers. In this step of the Process, you will specialize your labors, so that everyone in the Community is said to have one or more Functions in which s/he specializes and for which s/he gets Honored.

LAISSEZ FAIRE Vs. A SKILLS CENTER

When Laissez Faire is operating and everyone is doing just what they are accustomed to doing, it is not possible to coordinate efforts, nor to grow people from one functional area to another which demands a high degree of Education. This is to say, there is no way to train occasional volunteers to be midwives, managers, planners, or decision-makers. All these functions require full-time, dedicated people to work them.

As a result, a Laissez Faire Community will never progress beyond an aggregation of common interests and Good Times. It will never achieve Synergy, Growth, Abundance or Longevity.

SETTING UP A SKILLS BANK

To set up a Skills Bank [and later on, a credit union] your Community will need several decks of index cards and someone whose primary responsibility is seeing to it that members record essential data for the coordinator; and that's all. A computer is not necessary nor wanted.

FUNDING A COORDINATOR

Where the money comes from to engage a full-time coordinator is from the fund or bank checking account which runs cooperative purchasing. That function ought to generate a normal 5% surplus on purchases on each transaction, as well as add Member contributions in the form of contributed neighborhood collateral, member shares in the legal corporate entity, and free will donations earmarked for Community start-up.

A Synergy that begins to make this Fund grow is the savings people retain by buying corporately. Therefore, the primary purpose of the Skills Bank is to ensure that the Fund is well managed.

COOPERATION AS A FORM OF BEING ACCOUNTABLE.

There needs to be cooperation between the Manager of Collateral and the Spiritual Leader of this Community -- these two people must compete against each other and be mutually accountable. That tension is very healthy for the community -- like two sprinters setting the pace in a race.

During the Buying Process.

This is achieved by permitting each one to look over the shoulder of the other, and by essentially giving each of them the Same Deal, as above. That's how, they compete; and they alternate their years of service, so that both of them do not step down at the same time. (Do not leave an officer in one position for life; that begets corruption.)

By this time, the Group or Neighborhood has chosen a Way of Being, a Name, and a Mission. It's either skill-based, religious or ideological, or it won't fly. There has to be some primary motivation or devotion that a community is focused on and feels responsible for, or everybody just goes their own way. They're not inter-dependent in any way unless they're all working for the same goals, whatever those goals are.

This Book has illustrated two basic types of communities : one based a behavioral model and the other based in a religious devotion. I didn't go into ideology; that doesn't interest me.

A SKILLS BASE

A Skills Base can be either simple or complex. Simplicity means that it is a list of KNOWN individuals, their access locations, and what they know how to do competently. Temporary members require more information; guests need screening at the organizational and personal levels, in these times, sorry to say.

If you have a computer, you're not going to be using it classifying the Residents; indeed, no. You will be doing background checks on new people; and you'll have to get good at interpreting indifferent and institutional information. These are strange times.

Having no formal accounting system, except for sales tax and unavoidable cash expenses by your "cover business" also means the Tax Man has almost nothing to look at.

If everybody who happens to be at the Retreat Center this week is a volunteer, and volunteer jobs switch around, there are no wages to account for except for the Coordinator and the Inventory person. See where this goes? Sharing and giving among yourselves takes the place of income, and the tax bite goes away.

More complex means that there are job orders to fill, hour-for-hour trades to set up, and strict equivalent rules to follow. In the case of a complex system, it becomes very difficult to charge off labor at a rate of Minimum Wage or less, for tax purposes. And if volunteers insist on earning large numbers of dollars, Uncle Sam is going to want to take 20-30% of the total payroll, and that is a steep penalty for the Ego-gratification of earning high-dollar wages, especially if all one's Essentials can be acquired without any cash money at all.

But you and your group have got to learn to keep your heads down and lay low, financially.

The reason the subject of hourly wage comes up in such earnest at a skills center is that outside contractors Love to hire skilled workers out of your skills center, literally for peanuts, when the community gets to the point that jobs become options -- not requirements.

And at a point that contractors are knocking on the skills center door, the tax man is also probably waiting, hat-in-hand, for his 20-40% cut off the top of wages; and then you lose all your volunteer workers to cheap outside jobs. That's a problem. PLUS the added burdens of tax filing, preparation, detailed record-keeping and advance payments. So, leave money alone, except for taxes and Internet service; and find other ways to "deal," or the money lenders, property assessors, utilities and local agents will be at your door with their hand out.

My point is, there is no way to predict which way tax laws are going to go. But if "wages" for one or two employees are kept low and labor is kept within the Community itself, then everything should be all right and remain stable. NO MORE than a FEW [10% tops] individuals can work outside--so long as the Community is adequately staffed and comfortably housed--before jealousy sets in and competition, and bad feelings, and problems.

A DAY'S WORK

Mammals like lions and cows sleep 16-20 hours a day. I get zonked after six hours work because I'm intensely focused. And the workday in a Town such as this---with all the tertiary socializing that goes into it--cannot exceed 4 or 5 hours a day maximum, at least not for very long.

So the person who knows what skills are where needs to be organized around the assumption that everyone who works only does a 4-5 hour shift; and that there are always two shifts of people to take on any full-day task. That way, with everything double-booked with help, Things Get Done because people feel like doing them together, or they get done because people want to get this finished and go back to something else. But they get done.

WORKING ARCHETYPES

Just as different species of animals operate on different 'clocks,' people operate from different working archetypes. So far as we can identify, there are about fourteen archetypes people fall into, that determine their working styles. So, the Community needs to adapt its tasks to the working styles of the people who show up. The fact is, everyone will not do the same job in the same manner.

There are fourteen working Archetypes that serve in any Village, town or organized community. These are elaborated upon at page 152 and following

Having Respect for human archetypes and operating from Fairness, the Skills Center coordinates tasks and motivate people to meet objectives. Yet they must never push, only Pull Things Along by their own Good Example.

RECAP ~*~ So, let's recap where we are.

We have one person running the Tools and Equipment Service full-time (on a fixed income); another swapping and trading Stuff at flea markets to accumulate Collateral (part-time); and a Third person running the Co-op (part-time). At this point, Everybody else is still living entirely by the money economy, but they are beginning to realize some benefits of giving and receiving Promises, buying cheaply in volume, and working together to distribute staples and plan for the Future--PERHAPS-- their Own Community Village, with a Name and a Place and the beginnings of a History.

The Co-op is putting money in the Treasury; so are individual members who want to be able to get loans from the Collateral group, to build homes in a new and permanent location.

What this stage implies, now that everyone in the Community has begun to take on real jobs is that the time is come to finance Development, a Community infrastructure and Homes. Now comes the time when people -- if you'll excuse the expression--put their money where their mouth IS.

By this time, the Collateral Group has maxed out what it can raise in terms of leverage. By this time, the people who want to live together have already been looking at FREE or CHEAP land. [It must run less than $100 per acre so Development gets funded.] And they are putting up their homes for sale. What is true is that land exchanges will always be a feature of community life. The need for financing will always be present. The need for a safe place will always exist.

Collateral Accounts Converts to Pawn Shop Treasury

When everyone begins selling their present home in order to move to the Group Site, what becomes necessary is to conserve all cash. Conserving cash is accomplished by ten separate principles:

*Neglect is always more expensive than buying something really extravagant that does the job.

*Hopelessness is always revealed by the way people deal with money: the more money people waste, the less they feel Worthy.

What's Real is that providing Experiences in the Physical is more Holy than providing Things. Going skiing is less of an extravagance than buying a car, or a boat, or a second home. For most people, conforming to a Goal is truly a hidden way of conforming to other peoples' expectations. Free Spirits don't need to Shop, Shop til they Drop.

*Although the doctrine of Money is presumed to be Sacred, money doesn't exist in this Galaxy except on this Planet.

*Providing Money is >not< the same thing as providing attentiveness or caring. No one else can love your family as well and as competently as you can.

* When your life is finished here, the Experiences you have had will convey, but the things you have bought, won't.

*Integrity doesn't work where money is abundant; integrity works where money is scarce and Love is abundant. Gratitude isn't exchanged when a person is busy counting up his own gifts.

*Receiving conserves your energy so that one can give more. This means that believing you will Get has NO power, but believing that you will GIVE is very powerful, in attracting Good to you.

*If you count your chickens before they hatch, they will never hatch.

"The Pawn Shop" is what we call a place to Yield one's Things, to reduce them to Cash, AND it is where the Community's money must be stored safely. The person who operates the Pawn Shop (the Treasurer, if you like) cooperates with the Manager of Collateral, to see to it that all Community members are able to raise enough cash to get sufficient materials to build their homes in Community.

All collateral and possessions that can be sold at this point, are sold outside the Community to raise cash; and it will serve to Develop the Community's Toe Hold.

Principles for Cashing Out One's Possessions [without regrets later] --

The way one cooperates with experience is to cash out possessions no longer needed or used.

Sustaining Life is never the Issue; when one sells out mere Stuff, the Issue for selling it is to Facilitate Change and Growth.

Restoring a house or buying another USED house is always a waste of money. Homes age with their People and must be completely re-built for a new family.

A chance to uphold one's Initiation into Service for Humanity is a Good Reason to liquidate.

The death of a family member is another good time to liquidate some things. But never liquidate the things of a child that dies; always pass them on to extended family's children and use them until they wear out naturally. Death must **not be** a fearsome thing to the children left behind. But always liquidate the Things from a marriage that fails, so people can get on with their lives.

Immobilized people always attach to more Stuff than mobile people do. For that reason, the

Community should encourage people to have Yard Sales and Flea Markets regularly.

Conforming to the Goals of the Community needn't mean that a person CANNOT collect or liquidate special things -- stamps, coins, potsherds--which are not culled or put on display.

Finally, what is Sacred is upholding Harmlessness. Noisy guns and ammunition (that alarm neighbors) are not appropriate for selling in a community devoted to Peace; but a bow-weapon devoted to hunting an occasional deer in winter months can change hands without much fanfare.

The way to establish the People's Treasury is simple. Let the people give all their cash money to the Treasurer, and s/he puts it all together.

No notice is made of Who Gives How Much. If the Intention of the People is to sustain the Will of the Community, then it doesn't much matter which piece of cash serves what function.

Once the Community is built and furnished, then people will do outside work for pocket money.

Now, however, following the leadings of Community means that people must invest everything they happen to have in its infrastructure.

Members--because they have cast their bread upon the waters--can also expect that all their real physical and emotional needs will be met, yet while they have no cash reserves whatsoever. This is The Way a Developing Community must invest in itself, before it can function as a town. What happens later is what happens later.

And this is why a Newcomer who has not invested in the Beginnings of the Town will always be a Newcomer; why towns coalesce when the people who invested in it at first, come and dissipate when the Founders go.

Towns which learn to hang-on from generation to generation are often quite stagnant and immobile. If what we are saying about adaptability of towns is true, if what people tend to do is to want to establish a town of their own in their lifetime and leave the town behind when they die, then the outcome of this Reality is that Free Land is Essential.

The development and adaptation of Free Towns gives each Generation the opportunity to establish its Own Towns, so long as the land is never disrupted too much.

That is how tribal lands of Native Americans were operated for generation after generation, until white people took over and taught everyone to treat land as if people could own it.

People who want the Planet to Thrive as well as themselves will not pretend to own the Land; they will simply utilize and enjoy the land during their lifetime, and they will form legal covenants

that will provide that their children can do likewise: live Freely on FREE land.

For example, Google "Perpetual Land Trust" What Man can now take from Native American culture is their learned ability to live transparently, to pool their resources, and to only leave footsteps behind. For another example, Google The Rainbow People.

Recycling, Refurbishing and Crafts Center

This is a good time to talk about the presence and long-term effects of technology on the ecosystem, on the ability of the People to travel to the Stars, and on the Towns where people want to live with their families, bear children, age and pass on.

If someone were to claim that God doesn't support space travel, then the question arises: How does He Himself get around?

If God Himself is a Space Traveler and if He supports space travel for humans, then HOW--with simple technology as the town concept implies--will people ever travel out there to the Stars? The fact is, simple technology built the pyramids. Simple technology built up electronic theory [Tesla and Edison]; and simple technology will be the basis for space travel--not overblown NSA bureaucracy--just clarity, just ingenuity, just people working together.

It's already happening. In California there is a group of amateur rocket hobbyists who are working on a project to orbit their own space craft, as we speak.

What relevance has Space Travel to a Town? Modern Technology is a veritable **storehouse** of Waste! Many of the people who come to live in money-free Towns will do their share of The Work by salvaging what wasteful people thoughtlessly discard:

* metal engines, shafts and wheels, panels, hardware, tools; tires (for retaining walls)

* old hand-operated machining equipment, sewing, carding, weaving, sorting, moving.

Folks today toss out technology--without thinking--that took thousands of years to dream up, millions of dollars to build, and which will require a million years or more to compose back into the ground. So, why not just RE-USE materials you find lying around?

A Town Center for Recycling, Refurbishing and Crafts will be the HUB of activity for people whose Clarity resides with Things: salvaging, re-engineering, re-working, adapting. Everything salvageable which is not contaminated with Death or Disease is an opportunity to build up the town, so long as there is a person on board who knows what to do with it. If there are woodworkers in your Town, then salvage old furniture. If there are have metal workers, then salvage cars and machines. If there are electronics techs, then salvage computers.

But, never get what you can't fix up or trade and profit from. Just housing junk is not profitable. A good re-cycling and refurbishing Center will be the third continuous Work Place in Town. It should probably be located in close proximity to both the Tool Bank (for access to different kinds of tools) and to the Co-Op (where Free and Nutritious lunches can be served to men working).

This Work Place, however, will require extensive Storage Facilities, to warehouse junk, nonrenewable materials and recyclables that may not be used now, or for decades--yet must remain close at hand. Probably the best way to deal with that problem is to build a bunker-like below-grade storage facility, and berm it all around with mounds of grass and greenery, so it is not visible, and neither detracts from the ambiance of the Town itself nor puts recycle-able metals at risk of being stolen.

On the other hand, all crafts-people can work out in the open in public view because Visitors will want to participate, buy and trade with creative craftsmen.

Remember, always structure and lay out your Town so its Best Foot is in view; and its necessary Parts are out-of-sight of Visitors, who come with Cash and Goodwill.

VILLAGE--BUILDING

The Purpose of the Laws of God is to teach Awareness of Causes and Effects; of Justice; of Fairness. The Purpose of laying out a Town before you build it is to Get Past the Inertia of Distance and Time.

Making Work Easy has the same Effect as Not Being Dependent on Working. Specifying where Functions need To Occur is the Same as Having a Large Effect with a Small Movement.

Finally, linking all the parts Together with a Single Sustaining Road is the same as Intending that Opportunities will Succeed.

PREPARATIONS

To recap: you have money in the treasury from cashed out collateral.

You have purchased 100-200 covered plastic garbage bins to ease the Transition from a money economy to Freedom [for 50 people]. You have found FREE waste Land that has a watershed. [Wells are risky.] The Land must be hilly-at-least for drainage, for privacy. Flat Land is dangerous to live on, open and vulnerable.

You have left your house, and you have left all your nice things with others for safekeeping until the Road is built and your Tent is at Rest.

There will be a Gathering when you Reclaim your Good Life Stuff, later.

YEAR ONE--March through November

You must locate a Great Source of crushed rock, stones, and gravel; or concrete.

You must have moved your Tools, Books, and scavenged building materials onto the land, in tents and caves on higher ground, away from water.

Your temporary Co-op tent is set up on High Ground, and all foodstuffs are stored away.

(Caves are best; shaded, sealed garbage bins, okay) and protected from heat, bugs, and animals.

The people are now housed in trailers and tents, near the Co-Op and Work Groups.

There is a Tent for young children and a Tent for older children; and it is the work of an older child is to teach a younger one how to behave, one-on-one. There is a bathing Tent for men and one for women.

You must now dig all your latrines over the hill so that, when flooded, they runoff in the direction AWAY from the Town water supply, which is Holy.

There must be plenty of good-tasting, natural food to feed the workers, so they do not get sick working in Rain and Mud four hours a day; so you must have sufficient money to buy staple foods for everyone for 18 months, amounting to a total of ten sacks of grains/nuts/beans per person for that time period.

During Spring, the rainy season, you all can see how the watershed works, and you must adapt yourselves to its way.

You must capture all the fresh drinking water you can, in clean plastic garbage bins, with lids on them. Eventually, you will build cisterns.

If well water is available, cap it off for now; or test it daily for pollution and diseases.

Plan to capture and keep five gallons of rainwater per person per rainy day, until your water system is in place.

IT IS AT THIS POINT THAT YOU MUST DESIGN THE ROAD--NOT BEFORE, NOT LATER.

Remember, you are here to learn to GET OUT OF THE WAY of Trouble and Pain. Your Road will either make it Easy for you or Hard for you to Live.

It will take a year to build this road, with all the Help you can muster. After that, everything Else will seem Easy.

Model your land from a topo map and clay until everyone can see where the Road must go. To Reach Everything, to circle around and Come Right Back to where it started.

Hire a professional surveyor to mark out its boundaries in their Right Places, so the Road will be Upright and Level, not suffering from Washout.

This is going to be your greatest capital and labor output expense--ever.

THE THEORY OF ROAD BUILDING

Roads are built on your world as a convex curve that drains water off the edges. This is inappropriate, unsafe, and wrong to build.

Rethink how a road needs to be built. A road, to be safe, needs to travel One Way Only, in a circle, so it's Easy to get back to the Beginning. That way, the road only needs to be seven feet wide-->not< twenty-feet wide.

That way, the road does not intrude into the landscape, and it is invisible from the air, where trees tower overhead. This is good.

Being unobtrusive means the Tax Man does not Notice your comfort.

RAMPING A ROAD

A CONCAVE road runs water down the center of itself, particularly if a deep center trench is filled with large stones to permit water to drain easily.

But what is best about a concave road is that turn-overs are rare; ground covers are not In The Way; staying to the center of the road is Natural and Easy; the absence of on-coming Traffic makes the Road Safe, the Road takes up little space, fewer materials; and it is easy to keep.

BUILDING A ROAD FROM SCRATCH

An efficient road must consist of Loops that return to Center. It must accommodate Drainage, scraping of snow, and be weed-free. The way to accomplish all these criteria is to utilize crushed Rock, Layer upon layer, wheel barrow load by wheel barrow load.

Where the Center Drainage Trench is dug 12" across and braced with blocking stones (level with the road surface) that let water pass stone-filled, only the body of cars or wagons will pass over those stones; and hand-trucks move two-abreast.

From the large center rocks outward, new gravel can be added each year, to supplement what is already there. Ruts will be filled in with gravel. Washboards will be filled in with gravel. Pot-holes will be filled in with gravel. Weed-patches will be filled in with gravel. Drainage ditches will be regularly washed clear, to facilitate water flow and the gravel that gets washed down the center can be reused.

Plan for a full 12" of gravel to be finally built up, before the Road stays put. If more and larger rocks are needed to fill over an enclosed culvert, that works too.

The first winter is always hard. Some people will go home to families to wait out bad weather. Some people will hunker down in campers. Some will give up entirely. But the people who Stay, will Stay Forever.

As the Road is built up, land nearby can be developed, even if the Circle is not yet completed.

Let a Jitney help people move around to their Places, even only going in half-circles. Eleven times a day, let it circle about, and bring people and materials and belongings, so cars are not e'en thought of. It's better to have one jitney for fifty families than a score of cars and buses. Now your Honored Places must be dealt with:

* Tool and Book Library

* Schools, Food Co-op

*and the Refurbishing Center [hidden stores of commodities and recyclables],

*Skills Coordinator's and Counting Offices all must serve within stones' throw of each other.

Churches will arise where the People sense What is Holy. Arts and Trade Shops will locate near the Center of Town. The Clinic and Hospice need to be where Quiet overrules Business.

When the People deal with Placement BEFORE construction begins, then they save themselves thousands of steps, hundreds of hours, myriads of minutes for companionship, for Art, for Play and for Reflection.

Let there be a regular time of Silence when everyone is assembled, to reflect on and visualize the Town in its Glory Days. And then, when Glory Days do arrive, It will be EXACTLY SO.

Seasonal Gatherings ... have a trade-off: they encourage Trade and Industry, but they also encourage Disease.

Fundamental transactions that promote Abundance always occur where People Gather.

Yet, this Script is being written in a time of Plague: AIDS, hepatitis, tuberculosis viruses.

Therefore, we will proceed with an Assumption that Disease and Hunger are at work.

Future Generations must not be undermined by failed Gatherings that were intended to Thrive the People, but stumbled due to sickness and contagion.

THE ETIOLOGY OF DISEASE

When a new virus emerges, that is Gaia's Response to crowding and filth (or some outside genocidal wish).

The Belief that Disease is exchanged where people are physically touching or breathing the same air is inaccurate, in and of itself, unless the air is actually being sprayed with chemical contagion. Generally, what makes disease progress is permitting germs and viruses to propagate in rotting, standing or cooling media.

In a context in which healthful *CLEAN* practices are adopted, diseases will not spread unless they are spread deliberately. In the current political climate, it is a good idea to build all social places "under glass" to preempt the spread of disease.

Diseases always change in time -- unpredictably.

In any case, remaining focused on keeping things clean and germ-free is always good Practice, to keep everybody free of infection. Isolaing people who have Dis-ease is always good Practice also. Mating appropriately is good Practice. Matng to breed and rear strong children is one good goal; but mating for love and restoration of the Soul is another. And in either case, cleanliness and discipline inhibit the spread of diseases.

STAYING UNINFECTED

Before a Gathering can take place, latrines must be dug downstream from the Gathering Area. Another possible approach is to by portable "johns" which then must be truck-carried and unloaded into dug latrines that are downstream. Whether people use johns or dug latrines, is a matter of the preferences and resources of the community. Johns require chemicals that do the same job as strong vinegar and overripe tomatoes, to deodorize and break down fecal matter. Think about it.

The same latrines can be re-dug each year without odor if food waste, compost and kitchen clean-up water suds solution] are thrown on top of human waste before it is filled back in at the end of a Gathering. By next year, the soil will smell sweet once more because the soap and bleach will break it down. This is because fly eggs cannot live in the presence of bleach and soap, but worms can.

HYGIENE

To share meals with others, each single person or Family must bring 3 buckets, soap, chlorine bleach, bowls, cups, spoons and a knife to keep and use and be responsible for. If after each meal, everything is washed in soapy water in Bucket #1, rinsed in clear water in #2, and dipped in a 1-2 T. bleach solution in #3, disease will not spread. Then, throw soapy water and the bleach water into the latrine.

Every person must wash his or her hands with Soap AFTER using the latrine, digging in the garden, handling money, sneezing, picking their nose, or touching animals-- and BEFORE preparing food, treating a wound, making love, or touching another person's face.

Due to the prevalence of foot fungi, it is also good practice to scrub feet with a brush, soap and water and a 1T. vinegar to 1c water rinse

when one comes in from working in hot shoes or bare feet.

Dirty clothes incubate bacteria and odor. TAKE a bath and wash your clothes every day. Yes, I said BATH. Half a cup of baking soda in the bath will neutralize chemicals in the water, and you'll soak where you sit, clean. Showers leave the anal area reeking with bacteria.

ISOLATE THE DIS-EASED

Let's assume the worst: let's assume that your Gathering is taking place in the middle of a lethal epidemic. What can be done to protect the Healthy, and comfort the Afflicted?

1. First, each person who arrives feverish, tired, head-achy, upset stomach, in pain, with skin eruptions or emotionally disrupted--should receive and have set up from Stores : a pup tent, cot, blanket, towel, five gallons of fresh drinking water, and electrolytic supplements so they don't dehydrate and die.

2. If s/he has arrived alone, s/he is settled with other similarly Sick who help each other; If they arrive as a family, the family is charged with attending to them, keeping them clean and feeding them--at the north end of the camping area, so all the Sick are together, who have the same dis-ease.

3. If the whole family is sick and helpless, the family is settled at the furthest edge of the

Gathering, downstream and downwind, and accommodated with any Volunteer help that may happen to turn up for them. (monks and nuns may respond to calls from sick visitors, out of a vocation to serve God's Will.)

4. When the Gathering matures, good practice dictates that the host village build a weatherproof shelter for just such occurrences.

5. The sick are fed off paper plates and cups, and everything they use is collected in large paper bags and burned.

6. They are bathed by their parents, siblings, children or volunteers as often as need be; and their clothes in the tub with them, with bicarb of soda and warm water, so their clothes can be handled safely afterwards.

7. Their Clothes washed in lye-soap are hung out in the sun to dry; and the Sick One is provided with a simple chemise to wear and alternate with their own clothes, for each washing up, until the Gathering is ended.

8. No one who is sick may sleep with anyone else, except at the supervised Clinic..

9. If a Healer or others want to come to lay hands on the Sick for Healing, that is an option.

10. If the Sick are still Sick at the end of the Gathering, a Judgment can be made that Karma [Cause and Effect] is at work, and the Town must

provide for the Sick until they can all Go Home, to their Families or to God.

GATHERINGS, ROMANCE AND MATING

1. Familiarity breeds.

2. Relationships that begin in secrecy and sin reap a karmic cost of dissolution later on. Or, they result in a karmic pregnancy that people want to terminate, because destruction is never a blessing; Life is not the problem.

3. Plagues that exist are primarily sexually-transmitted.

4. For people who are already married, Gatherings are a business opportunity, a discipline.

5. For people who are single, Gatherings will advertise not only their physical prowess or beauty, but also highlight obsessions, confusion and alienation at work.

6. Thus, Gatherings are a test of character for all participants..

SEXUAL ACTIVITY AND DISEASE

1. Sex is messy, and not an appropriate activity for Public Display.

2. Sex has health and breeding consequences that can mar a person's experience. And if a failed romance yields unwanted pregnancy and

the necessity to decide to accept a child or abort it, ". . . a lack of family commitment between sexual partners who breed without regard for costs or outcomes causes problems in any village. Abortion may be a short-term merciful end to a harsh experience of childhood, but it is not an experience that we abide with or favor. What is preferable is to place such a child for adoption by Law-abiding parents in a Lawful Community, to be reared as a potential Ascender, for most Ascendants tend to come from mixed backgrounds, and they have very difficult and troublesome youth experiences.

3. Everybody knows who doing what with whom. You're all psychic anyway, so there's really No Way to 'get away with it' at a Gathering.

4. Let that be so. Let Vitality serve as an End in Itself and not in more troubles.

5. People who become Friends at Gatherings can take up a more serious relationship at a later, more appropriate time.

~ G A T H E R I N G S Miracles in the Making ~~

The Law Abides with Love by sharing, thanksgiving, and evoking natural profits (prophets). This Planet was set up to express the gifts of free will and manifest Miracles.

When all humans are educated in integrity, then free will and manifest miracles provides for everyone, without servitude (as on Saturn's Moon *Titan*, even now.)

God never intended that people should be subject to the rules of impersonal Entities.

Today People have few options to exchange or trade values and skills because everything they do is attached to money and taxation and because counting pennies is favored over counting favors, gifts, and love. Buying and selling are limited to Corporate Rules.

YET we insist: God provides. Here is the Way business is done where free will and miracles are permitted to manifest.

THE SEASONAL GATHERING A Place of Tent and Meeting *

Competence and cooperation are taught; delight itself provides a way of change, and the people open themselves to new tools and knowledge. We call this Gathering a Free Gathering because admission is not an issue; only the costs incurred in traveling and setting up camp and business with food to share and to spare--fall on Participants.

Camp space, water, sanitation, staple foods, emergency care, child care and Entertainment are all part of the Program. So is Voluntary Helping Out and Cooperating with the Rules, part of the Program. Disruptions are not part of the program, so you must have a group devoted to Security details.

PREPARATIONS

Preparations are based on an Expectation to competently handle ten times a Town's population.

First, a count needs to be taken, of the number of people who are working to cooperate.

Each activity needs to be arranged so hundreds of people can sit down comfortably and see it. What will profit everybody is if Every Visitor has a Good Time.

The people who are going to present and perform at the Gathering need to come forward and be counted.

Everyone needs to be able to hear what speakers and performers are saying and singing; sound systems will need to be set up.

A Stage Crew needs to know when and where things will have to be brought up and taken down.

Competence shows in preparation, in the presence or absence of music, lighting, and program.

Free Spirits are always open to suggestions; so is a FREE Gathering, open to suggestions and assistance; but staffing also has the freedom to intervene, to bring a behavior to a halt, or to oust (with help) disruptions from their midst.

Keeping everyone healthy is a primary consideration or the Gathering will have a bad outcome.

THE MAIN ATTRACTION

The main feature of a Gathering is giving people a reason to mingle, relate, and sense what is Holy, Sacred, Real, Necessary and Beautiful. Thus a Gathering can deal with anything contained in the sum of Life that people favor.

This is where peoples' works find acceptance and a ready market. What is appropriate at a Gathering is whatever is safe and interesting, whatever deals with awareness--of time, of beauty, of sound, of harmony--is On Display.

Opportunities to "Try It Out," "Try It On," "Open It Up," and "Look At That" are all around you.

What happens is that individuals evoke feelings, manifest desires, make agreements, and wake up their spirits. And the will bears all things, with grace and candor. This is a good discipline.

MIRACLES ARE A PUBLIC SPECTACLE.

The Miracle that everyone will witness is the miracle that everyone who comes today gets their needs met, without money and without price.

First, individuals with "items to give, share or swap" come up on stage to talk about what they brought; and they get a round of applause for their generosity; then they are sent out to the booths to have their gifts counted and their Promises filled out and witnessed to. [And then they come back in at the Front.]

Individuals with "services they perform" for people are called on stage to tell about their Services; and after they get a round of applause for offering their skills, they are sent out to the booths in Back to have their Promises drawn up, which they can commit to fulfill. [And then they come back in through the Front, if they have more to offer.]

Individuals with "Helping Out skills" (e.g., care-giving, housekeeping, maintenance) come forward to offer their help; and when they receive a round of applause for their diligence, they are sent out to the Booths in back to have their Promises scheduled and so they can spend it them elsewhere. [And then they come back in the Front to witness the rest.]

Some people have now been on stage receiving applause THREE TIMES--and they are hyped. They have stuff, they have skills, they have time to help. Now it's time for obtaining the experience of obtaining.

Selecting who gets their preferences first is simple: the One with the largest number of promises outstanding WINS!

[Most people already have in mind what it is that they WANT; they're just looking for the source of their wishes. Now we are going to make it easy for them to get what they truly want.]

And the first one who WINS must speak his/her Fondest Wish. And everybody in the audience looks around to see who or where this wish might be hiding. And then someone will yell out, 'I've got one for you!'

And then it moves to the next one with the most tickets; and that one tells his or her fondest wish; and again, everybody in the Audience looks around to see who or where this wish might be hiding.

And then someone will yell out, 'I've got it for you!' [It never fails. In this type of crowd, some-one always does GOT ONE.]

And on and on it goes, until the only people left are the ones who have no Promise currency, nothing. They came unprepared, or alone, or whatever.

So the Master of Ceremonies says, 'Now we will see a miracle for those without money and without price!' [These are the people who are sick or afflicted, or new, or scared.] "Come ON down! you who brought nothing with you!" All these people are brought together on Stage [while the

ones with Money are busy bargaining and trading their Promise Currency].

And some light music is playing. while the Participants are trading their currencies, they hold a little back, just in case someone is In need in that final group.

Then the Pastor/ Prophet/ Guru/ Seer comes into the middle of the (very embarrassed) group of individuals standing on the stage, and he invokes a blessing upon them saying, "What you give unto others, will be given unto you. What do you have in your pocket or purse that you can give?"

So the hapless people left on stage bring out a handkerchief, or a roll of Tums; and the new person brings out a little money [because they still live by money], and the scared person brings out a lucky charm.

And each one puts their token into a colorful hat.

And then each one is asked if they have seen something they liked or wanted or needed in all the program.

And they'll always say, Yes, they did. So whatever that WAS will be given to them; and all that is asked of them is the token from their pocket. Thus Everybody Wins.

And then the Pastor/ Prophet/ Guru/ Seer gives an Invocation, and everybody goes to the Dining Tent for a light meal and the Gathering is Complete. Most communities can only sustain one such Gathering in a year; and the people will begin working on the Next Year's Gathering the week after this one is over.

This is the end of the module devoted to Living Without Depending on MONEY.

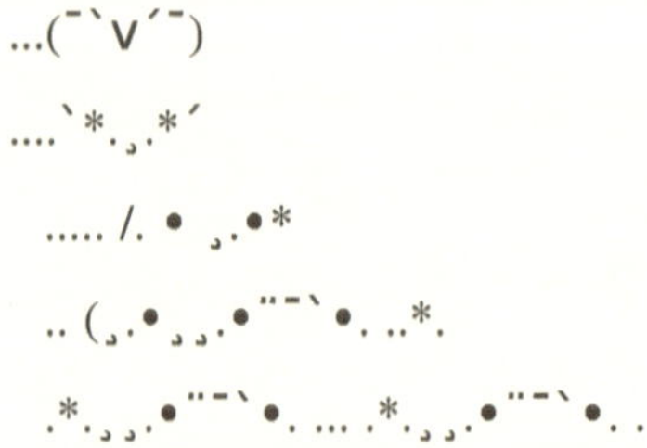

THE SPIRITUALLY REDEEMED HUMAN LIFE

How Peoples practice their lifestyles will either thrive a land or strip it barren.

Harmlessness works as a form of Clarity that looks at Effects and Outcomes.

What is Just is that every person's physical and spiritual needs must be met.

What is Fair is that every person must bear his or her share of the Work.

What is Necessary is that Peoples must look out for each other without profiting, because money itself is a very expensive and extravagant tool.

That implies that people must become aware of each other's necessities and deficiencies.

Moreover, most people will have to confront the decision to which Community to attach because it is very difficult to be totally self-sufficient in isolation.

No one will experience the redemption of living simply who doesn't actively seek to build and be part of community.

There is nothing automatic about building community, and it takes a lifetime of devotion to bring one into being.

"RIGHTNESS" EXPRESSED AS SACRED EFFECTS

What Does God Hope To Gain By the Salvation of Human Lives and Memories?

866---The function humans need to fill is to guide and adapt their Goals to Spirit direction.

663---Spirit Direction is a learned skill, not instinctive nor based entirely on Reason.

360---Seeing Coherence in All Reality forms a Way to find God in what looks like Chaos.

060---What appears chaotic must be articulated as Prayer, so that God can deal with it.

070---Sensing what's Real and reckoning what's Fair serve only as Perspectives from which to operate.

080---One must learn to detect the Line that Justice takes through what's Fair and what's Real.

091---Life has patterns, but they must not become carved into Stone. Instead, the Initiate transcends patterns -- family, culture, star signs, archetypes and roles.

101---What works is Inner Discernment of the significance of the Outer World.

111---What is felt is Safe is also what is Appropriate to move on.

121---Physical life is about dealing with listening, awareness, with intuition. Everything else is mere distractions and noise that lead to more Chaos.

131---Physical Life is about being open to trying things out, just for the experience.

141---Physical Life is about being whole-souled, focused and engaged in life, not merely watching.

151---Each person must bear his/her Gifts with Grace and produce Fruits in due season.

161---Physical Life is about articulating one's experiences, Inner and Outer.

171---Each person must look to find his/her own Understanding, own Reasons, own Judgments.

181---What's Good produces harmony; what's bad produces obsessions, guilt and harm.

192---Thinking itself is either a good practice or a harmful practice, depending on where it leads.

202---Participation and sharing are always choices which present themselves.

212---Participation with others is always easier when an individual is already aware of what comprises 'appropriate' dealings.

222---Commitments have a powerful effect on one's life; so they must not be taken lightly.

232---The commitment to Love is not based in conditions; Love endures all things.

~*~ SALVATION'S ELEMENTS ~*~

Salvation is an acquired characteristic; it is not inborn.

Salvation is a point-of-view that ebbs and flows.

A person has to take it and run with it, as in a relay race.

Salvation represents Standing in the Sight of God.

So long as the person conforms to God's Will, s/he retains that Standing.

Articulating Salvation is simply living a Life in God's View.

Life evolves. Sometimes individuals evolve with it; sometimes they give up.

God loves them either way.

Salvation has been misunderstood.

People think souls who get Saved are even those who practice sin.

If a person is practicing Sin or Evil, Salvation does not help them.

What Salvation means is that their memories are saved--in God's Memory.

If the memories are saved of a practicing criminal, then what does GOD REMEMBER?

On Resurrection, that one will remember how to commit crimes, and will do it again.

Hell is the place where all memories of Crimes, Sin and Evil are forgotten.

Hell is not knowing who you are [or were], so you can Start Over Fresh.

Hell is memories of Crimes, Sins and Evil deleted, and starting off with a new fresh file disk.

Hell is not bad. Lack of recognition of who you were is not bad.

What serves God's Purpose to evolve Thought is Fundamental: God deletes bad memories,

So stop trying to save all your criminals. Let them go. God will erase all their memories so they start over Fresh -- not burdened with guilt and evil strategies from the Past.

Let Evil Go. Let Evildoers go. Let Sin go. Let Sinners go.

God will correct these matters if you do not perpetuate problems by 'trying to save their Souls' this time, as if failure this time means failure forever.

This is not so. God loves All the Souls, even those who practice sin, for the Good they also DO. Everyone does some Good. It is sufficient.

~*~ LIVING BY Holy LAW [Essene] PRINCIPLES, as Jesus DID

9890--Reckoning Law and Maintaining Law DIFFER

Reckoning the Law implies a relationship between Law and Good Effects.

Maintaining Law demands new relationships built on Trust that must find reasons to hold the Law Sacred.

Law is always corrupted by "traditions" not contained

nor implied in Laws Moses gave.

What the Jews DID was justify preferences over centuries of experience, by a judicial process that became sacrosanct as if from God.

What they should have done was infer what is Holy [Fundamental to Life], Sacred [Harmless], Real [of Value] and Active in each generation anew.

YHVH will now set the Law straight, so What is Lawful and What is Holy is the Same Thing.

In the matter of the Sabbath: The Purpose of the Sabbath is the Rest of God, not merely the Rest of men. When human preparations take on the scope of 'a production' with a 'countdown,' then Sabbath is being staged for appearances.

This is not appropriate. The Sabbath calls for Simplicity and for the Experience of Simple Joys. All Effects that mimic Rest are just as pointless as the work they replace.

Two meat dinners per week are sufficient to strengthen the people and occasion gladness without diminishing the Women's Rest. Otherwise, meals can be very simple and straightforward.

A simple supper of roasted meat and steamed greens with a side-dish of beans or fruit is all that needs to occur for Friday Sabbath.

Bread is for meatless meals, not to be combined with meat at all. Put down elaborations, and let Women Rest, not just the Men.

A Kiddush can be composed each week anew from the Knowledge of the People without repeating the same menu over and over.

Let the children speak their knowledge of God and Glory in Safety. The People whose God is YHVH can spare the Time to let their children sing.

The matter of *Shul: Shul* is the delight of YHVH, because therein He sees the thoughts of His people together and in one place.

Let *Shul* Stand. Yet, use a modern translation of Scripture so learning the ancient and foreign language does not take up years of your time.

A sermon [or homily] should continue to balance wisdom and text with an up-to-date application to personal, communal and societal concerns.

Do not charge for services. Rather, let a meeting of the People produce Volunteers [in twos or threes] who willingly pay each obligation the Community incurs. That way, all tithes go to the poor, the fatherless and the foreigner among you who happens to be in need, and the Congregation never suffers from Glut or Luxury.

In the matter of Sacrifices: What is Lawful is that First Fruits are given to God.

What is Holy is that God gives the First Fruits to the Poor, to the Fatherless, the Widow, the Sick, the Outcast--NOT to the coffers of the already-fat who are priestly and prosperous.

Let them fast this day, and others enjoy God's Gifts. Let the Shoe Be On The Other Foot, when the Lonely get YHVH's bounty first.

In the matter of *Kashrut: it* teaches Compassion. Yet fish and fowl are also meat, and need to be included in *Kashrut*, not left out.

Ritual slaughter teaches the Sanctity of Life. Let your animals never sense the Fear of Death; and only kill for sufficient meat for Sabbath [Friday night and Saturday noon] and winter meals.

You must exclude all 'bottom-feeders' from your selections of clean fish, due to pollution and weakening of the Kinds. Wild Flounder and wild ducks are becoming too dangerous for eating; yet farmed, these are fine.

Although Technology may in other respects fix the problem of food and sanitation, now having one set of dishes that is GLASS [for everyday] and one set of dishes that is China [for your Sabbath meat meals] is sufficient.

Iron pots are for cooking grains and dairy [which are thereby imbued with needed heme iron]; steel pots are for cooking meat [which are sanitary and easy to *kasher*].

Let your children [until age 21] have meat and milk on the Sabbath, milk with grains the rest of the week.

In the matter of Attire: No Chaste or Lawful person shaves their hair or beard, as a sign on their countenance of their Covenant relationship. But if the practice of sin leads to being cut off [being shunned], then that one's braid is cut off also, as a sign to the nations.

Head coverings serve to identify a person's Role, an Activity, a Safety Measure for long hair, or an Event. Lack of a Covering also alerts Sentinels in a Community, that NOT everyone present has a Role to fill.

But FREE WILL is also present for the freedom of motion that comes with the breeze and the rain and the wind in one's hair. Let not dogma or doctrine dominate over commonsense when people are at play and rest. What is also Lawful is that *tzit tzit* remind the People of their Existence as Lawful Jews. Let All the People wear the *tzit tzit,* not just the men. Let All the People dress simply, not copying the styles of the nations.

Let All the People adopt natural fabrics and colors, and forgo polluting dyes and bleaches.

Let Priests not injure the people by wearing what's Holy [and extravagant] attire, but allowing our people to repudiate what's Holy with chemical dyes that destroy the water-table.

If *tefillin* and *phylacteries* serve to focus a man on composing his prayers, then they harm nothing.

In the matter of Prayer: Formal, fixed times for prayers bless God; but the words don't come from the Heart, of what value are they? Take NOT your services out of Books. Let each leader or facilitator compose the Poetry that operates the Service, from the Wisdom of the Holy Spirit, anew.

Morning and evening prayers and Listening bring each person back to the Presence of God. This is Good. Anyone can read a prayer; mere Reckoning is working. But to compose a prayer--from one's own Sacred Perspective, from one's own Work Archetype, from one's own Experience, from one's own Feelings--this composition demands inspiration, Reasoning and Skill to be worth listening to.

Let People work from Reason and not mere Reckoning of rules and procedures. Let YHVH hear the True Nature of the People, not mere words of the Past. Let the men lead Prayer in *Shul* by their own Composition and Voice. Let the women lead Prayer at home [even in the presence of their husband] by their own Composition and Voice also.

Let Law-full People pray outright to YHVH, needing or having no Intermediary.

Because you are a Holy Nation, not a community of Sinners, your communities must carry the Karma of the Earth herself on your Shoulders; Yeshua does not carry your load for you.

So, Honor God with your voice of ***prayse***, of thanksgiving, of woe, of suffering; and YHVH your God will be present with you and teach you to reason from His store of wisdom, justice and mercy.

In the matter of Money: Although it was written that a Jew could not charge interest on a loan, the Jewish money-lenders have become proverbial creditors to the world. The karma from this effect is great; and the anger of nations against Jews is great.

From now on, no new Jew will loan money except interest-free. No economic system will arise due to the practices of the Kingdom of God, except that of seed money and creating a tenfold return to fund self-sufficiency alone.

No commissions or over-rides will accrue for doing what's simply expected, because you are a Holy Nation, not a community of Sinners. Tips are always appropriate because they reveal God's Will. The Law-Full of YHVH carry the karma of the Earth upon your shoulders; and yet even this must not be overly burdensome, as YHVH would have it. Sufficient prosperity accrues to those who work from a trade or skill, that manipulating money need not put one person or people over another or others.

In the matter of tithes: In the past, all tithes were given to the temple. The effect of this doctrine is to centralize wealth.

Centralizing wealth means people at the edge are cut off. Cutting them off serves to change behavior, to cope more lawfully or to retreat to ego.

Accountability

In the Past, secrecy of the Priesthood kept money in its control. NOW Let tithes and gifts become the Responsibility of your Management Office [whatever you call it] so all the Books are Opened and All the People can see to whom tithes and gifts are truly beneficial.

This way, no one will be left out, who has any Integrity or Standing in the Community, who may be poor or sick or suffering.

In the matter of backsliding: Let those who practice Sin among you be referred to a Christian Community to love one's neighbor as oneself until Godly behavior returns as regular practice. Christians practice repentance and redemption. Let sinners not become a permanent dole at a Community's expense.

In the matter of *Taharat Hamishpachah* [Family purity] : These are the days of pestilence ahead, when viruses follow unseen paths and lay low whole multitudes. *Taharat hamishpachah* is the Commitment to What is Holy, Sacred, Real and Active, not merely to physical preferences, expediencies and appetites.

Let *Niddah* [separation] for a woman continue for ten days each month, and then the woman should go get her *mikvah* at the Bathhouse [without money or price].

There, any evidence of infection or pregnancy can be observed and dealt with kindly.

What is Holy is Healing. What is Sacred is Accounting for disease. What is Real is taking Responsibility for its effects. What is Active is the Judgment of the *Mikvah* Lady, that blood tests are incumbent, or that a Doctor needs to be in attendance.

At the Bathhouse, women must practice all their Healing Arts: homeopathy, massage, yoga, acupressure--the list is long--for repentance and redemption of disease not to become a permanent burden by virtue of disability, at the Community's expense.

Also, may be be incumbent upon the mothers and brides in the community to have a network of skills to keep themselves happy and Holy in their Work and in their Lives. [This is WHY elaborate Sabbath preparations are not appropriate on Friday afternoons, so time for healing and regeneration is what works to prepare women for their husbands.]

Likewise, the men need their own sweat lodge, their place to make noise [undetected] each week, their own form of exercise discipline, their way to exchange the Peace of God, that does not have to answer to the convenience of the Women.

Then communities' and Peoples' festivals will take on a spirit of vitality of health and freedom, unencumbered by ease or satiety.

"VALIDATING" ONE'S SPIRITUAL LIFE ~*~

Three lifestyles -- AbideWith Favor (by Holy Law), Simple Faith (by Grace) and Anomalies (Oath Keepers) provide sufficient justification for a soul at death to be "saved" [memories stored]. A person following one of these ways of living is probably already responding to a type of spiritual direction.

Perhaps you have already noticed these archetypes in people whom you know. Naturally, they have not existed by accident, rather by God's desire to look fairly at experiences of diverse peoples.

95.75 Abiding with Favor -:- Jewish Covenant -:-

Some people willing to abide with Favor ["Holy Law"] already have a strong attachment to principle which is beyond reason.

Usually, it is a long-standing Karmic attachment; and it is most noticeable because a person who abides with favor always stands out from his natural family and friends as a real kook.

That's because characteristics that make for gentle human life and those that make up a prophet are incompatible. "Favor" in this case, means "challenge"--not indulgence.

Any person who is by nature a conformist will never make it as a Law-abiding prophet because what prophecy is about is telling the world what Yahweh wants to say, without regard for how people happen to like it or whether they want to hear it.

God's prophet must be highly or even, over-socialized, so they can speak with a level of clarity and tact their audience will detect as Spirit-driven.

The matter of Integrity is always at issue, because prophets simply do not take material matters very seriously in the first place, in the second place, or even in the third place. They are usually in a lot of hot water wherever they go, for not wanting to go along with the usual programs, rules or ways.

We chuckle over this and it fits our own experience. It is harsh to be one of God's own, because there are always many more claimants than there are "genuine articles." Cheap imitations are a dime a dozen, but the one who really listens to God is the one who will put up with anything, yes, anything, for the privilege of doing this work.

Abiding with Favor is tough. It's not fun, it's not easy, and it's not simple because the Almighty doesn't care whether a candidates likes it, is comfortable with it, or it's convenient.

Service to God simply is the way it is, take it or leave it. And this is how learning prophecy works for each Individual who takes it on.

Taking on a responsibility for prophecy can produce a justified status for an individual or for a whole community. This means, the residents' memories are saved, and God's Will regulates his, her, or their attachments.

Think about that. It means, the individual or the community relinquishes their Free Will, for the time they serve.

Whatever the Diet that an Initiate consumes is whatever God personally directs: local fresh foods, grain, beans, nuts, fruits, vegetables and dairy products.

Because Clarity of Thought is essential, no drugs are permitted; wine or beer are permissible on the Sabbath; caffeine is discouraged; nicotine is forbidden. Due to pollution and disease, blood and blood products are avoided, as well as placenta products, animal residues, and drugs designed to render a stupor or death including general anesthesia.

Black and/or white clothing only is worn, except on the Sabbath, when solid colors and embroidery are suitable as ornamentation. Hair and/or beard is uncut except when in service to a political entity. Hair is covered or a hat is worn when the Individual shows up in their Community Role. No community role means, no head covering.

Initiates do not work for money; work only for God and accept the income which results from that work, in or out of Community. They find a need and fill it rather than accept employment with rules attached.

If a person is married when commissioned as Abiding in Favor, they will have no additional children unless that is their directed path. If the person is single, they work toward autonomy with companionship, or they permit God to arrange for a marriage-companion, who must also follow the Abiding with Favor commitment.

Expectations around care of young children and of aged parents are to be included in the prayers and responsibilities of Prophets, so long as these responsibilities exist. Expect that the active ministry of God will begin however when these other responsibilities have naturally subsided.

The Will of the Almighty God is that all Beings--material, subjective, and cosmic--shall enjoy one day of rest out of seven: no working, no cooking, no studying, no buying, no intense discussions, just rest and relaxation. You can go to church or get married on any working day, because preparing for and attending church or a wedding is attending to business. However, a meditation, funeral, prayer- or healing-service IS Sabbath-appropriate.

It is expected that Initiates will associate with communities which likewise practice simplicity, integrity, and autonomy, for the purpose of learning cooperation, generosity, justice with mercy and compassion. But they do not need to tithe, just give as money arises. Receiving mercy requires that the abiding with favor individuals remain neutral in wars and politics.

The work of centering one's character is recognized as Just, and ***it is noticed and recognized that every human picks and chooses from the menu of ideologies and behaviors.*** Regulating what happens to arise to produce a consistently centered mental and physical state of is an appropriate practice for Abiding with Favor. Sustaining the primary attachment to God is required so that all guidance and discipline comes from God directly. This is accomplished by setting aside 2-3 hours each day for prayer, meditating, walks in the woods, primarily in silence.

Their relations among church communities will naturally reflect conflicts of interest and disrupt what is considered "normal" doctrines. This is good; it fosters self-examination.

Those abiding with favor are judged by the standards of all three judgment paradigms (Effects, Law and Mercy) together and separately. God is the God of Law and Order, so Individuals' work must conform to and promote God's Will. When the individual successfully sorts out his/her integrity consistently, this assignment becomes a cosmic one. Usually, by the time a person gets to this junction, he or she has been prepared well enough mentally that failure is not contemplated nor expected.

There are many abiding with favor candidates who have never moved beyond this point of following directions from God to full Ascender status. Most candidates tend to become stabilized as monastics. God's Mercy permits them to keep their status even though it has become clear that they will not initiate a move beyond this point in their development. They often become self-righteous, a characteristic shared with the angels; and the discipline of righteousness becomes a head trip and lacks heart energy. Defaulted initiates serve to articulate self-rightness and evil.

The experience of hyper-religiosity has no purpose. Religion that comprises form and ritual has no meaning. Only when ritual also symbolizes practice does it take on cosmic value.

94.74 Simple Faith

Simple Faith individuals do whatever is sanctioned in their Faith Community with respect to food, drugs, alcohol, caffeine and tobacco. What conforms to the Community's doctrines and rules is what is Holy for fundamentalists. When reason conflicts with doctrine, the matter becomes grist the the Church to decide, not for the individual to decide on his or her own.

They wear whatever the Community finds to be appropriate; hair and beard follow customs and styles, but head is not shaved clean, usually covered by a hat.

Many fundamentalists work for money to support self and family in a trade which does not degrade nor take advantage of others, and tithe to the Church to support its social outreach program.

A person of Simple Faith marries for life in the faith, as their Church finds appropriate and as they so choose. Often there are no provisions for divorce; freedom to use birth control or unite homosexuals, if those practices have been accepted and sanctioned by the Church and the Community of the Faithful, are options for those individuals with gender issues who want to practice a reverent form of family stability.

Family Expectations around the care of young children and of aged parents are included in the prayers and responsibilities of those of Simple Faith, so long as these responsibilities exist. Expect that many a Ministry of God will begin, however, when these other responsibilities have naturally subsided, because effective Ministers cannot serve Family and Congregation at once.

They observe a Sunday 12:01 am. to Monday 12:01 Rest Day, regardless when they attend their Church services.

Simple Faith people have Integrity which makes them favorable candidates for public political office; yet, their positions on issues may differ markedly, and they will take sides in controversies and wars.

Simple Faith individuals find a process in their worship group that restores erring people to their senses or releases them to the World outside. A person may go from church to church to find respite; yet if s/he is released from many successive churches for reprehensible behavior, that one will eventually remain outside the Faith due to being shunned.

93.73 Anomalous Individuals

Self-disciplined and Spirit-led individuals who attach--due to their interest in Cause-and-Effect, as gurus and teachers are guided by angels. They are vegetarians or not, work for peace and for the articulation of disputes and conflicts, which means, they usually stir things up.

They have a common point-of-view, centering on Agnosticism or a Natural Religion like Buddhism.

Anomalies often utilize natural psychedelics and suffer from their effects. They wear whatever the community finds to be appropriate, usually black and white, with or without tattoos, studs and chains. They tend to be hardy-looking, quite often shaving their heads instead of their beard. They may dye their hair any number of colors, for effect.

858---What brings praise is being able to initiate good ideas that are also workable.

868---Their function works from a single point-of-view, which they articulate in great detail. The Anomaly uses relationships as appropriate to promote and complete the work he/she is commissioned to do. Families are sacred; angels, likewise. The Anomaly then, promotes family ties over all other considerations. His families work to regulate and focus all family members on ego processes of headship and problem-solving based on dominance and submission.

878---They adapt to associates, and the context in which they live affects their decisions rather than greatly imposing themselves on others. They adapt.

888---Those who complete what they start are the ones who become leaders of spiritual movements. Spiritual teachings and religious practices of Anomalies will vary widely; however, they will be individualistic and ego-oriented in practice. Iconoclastic individuals are often apolitical, because angelic doctrines teach that war is failure of ego to keep the peace, not a continual struggle between Right and Wrong.

899---When their inner work is complete, they become candidates for ascension to Cosmic service as teachers and gurus, adopted by their students. Judging for himself that his work supports Good, the Anomaly does not work with anyone except on terms which promote ego. The Anomaly gives to the poor, the sick, and the wretched anonymously, not through established churches, a defining characteristic, usually focused on replacing social processes corrupted or inactive. Perhaps the work is military justice, crime detection or enforcement, profane art, music, law, technology or philosophy. Usually, people don't mess with Anomalies.

909---Then the world applies its Judgment to them and their life and teachings. Autonomous individuals are judged by the effects of their judgment experiences in the world, whether the sum total of their good outweighs the sum total of the bad, but their memories are not saved; they are not justified.

HISTORY IS PAST : Holy CAUSES ARE ETERNAL and Self-Sustaining.

The Path of God YHVH Employs Cause and Effect on a Heading toward Joy.

807--What is Holy is the Sense of Experience--IN- and not out-of-time.

797--It's the most fun if everyone's experiences can be included, that sufficed as Wise.

787--What's going on becomes associated as elements and relations to each other.

777--What's active must be what gets people excited and adapts them to keep going.

767--What's necessary is to gain all the perspectives that can be sincerely experienced.

757--It's a challenge to remember and store all this data; yet the Holy Spirit is Faithful.

747--Attachments form the dominant links for a long time.

737--Eventually, cooperation is what counts.

727--Finally, the people achieve and maintain moment-by-moment clarity and Truth.

717--When this occurs, Reason becomes prevalent in place of mere Reckoning or Rule-following.

706--Although Reckoning is what is spoken and written down for All to employ,

696--what is acquired is the sustaining power and flexibility of Reasonable-ness.

686--Some day, each Perspective will serve its own Function without Judging the Others.

676--Points-of-view are Eternally Necessary, simply to be able to communicate on common-ground.

666--Composing one's point-of-view demands goals and specificities.

656--Each point-of-view will acknowledge all the others' forms.

646--Each one will Stand and speak out from his or her own Role in material Life.

636--Teaching will exist as what is coherent with what.

626--Speaking one's own Truth will become comfortable and natural.

616--Thus, Life will become articulated, experience-by-experience, as long as it Lasts.

Causes and effects can be detected and discovered.

Any Effect which manifests and is judged Sacred has an integrity of its own.

Experience is the record of causes and effects in the Material.

Cause and Effect reveals what is of God ["of Good"] and what is temporary.

Expectations around Cause and Effect changes what actually occurs.

All final and summary effects include what is Essential and Of God.

Yet what is Essential is never THE Visible Part of an Effect.

FURTHER QUOTATIONS :

"Man only, of all the created animals, was created not perfect in his order, Saith Jehovih. The most devoid of knowledge, and most helpless of animals, created I man. I gave not to the bird to improve her feathers; nor yet to improve her species; nor gave I her a book as to the manner of building her nest, nor as to her behavior with other birds. Nor I said to the hare: Beware of foxes, or go thou, teach thy young to depend on their fleetness. And yet, both, birds and beasts, move by My inspiration, perfectly in the order I made them; the bird doeth her work, and the hare fleeth from the fox. But the child of man will put its finger in a serpent's mouth, and child will also eat any deadly poison.

"Thus differently created I man from all other things on earth; but I gave him the foundation whereon he might attain to perfection in all the attributes of My other living creatures. And I said to man: Be thou observant of what thou shalt eat and drink, and where thou shalt dwell by day, and sleep by night. For all things shall write upon thy soul the character and kind whereof they are made.

"If thou wilt be gentle, like a lamb, and non-resistant and docile, so thou mayst obtain great knowledge, feed upon herbs and fruits and cereals. And thy blood shall be pure and cool, charged with food for thy spirit, in peace and in love.

"If thy blood shall be hot, and thy spirit shall be stirred with passion and anger and contention and tattling and war and jealousy and love of vengeance, whatsoever thou chargest thy blood with, shall be charged upon thy spirit.

"Because thou canst not feed on fish nor flesh but through destruction unto death, even so, destruction unto death shall come upon thy soul. From thine own blood shall thy spirit be inspired, even according to what thy blood containeth." The ***OAHSPE***, Book of Inspiration, Ch. XII, page 822 copyright by John Ballou, New York, 1882).

"All religious philosophy, sooner or later, arrives at the concept of unified universe rule, of one God. Universe causes cannot be lower than universe effects. The source of the streams of universe life and of the cosmic mind must be above the levels of their manifestation. The human mind cannot be consistently explained in terms of the lower orders of existence. Man's mind can be truly comprehended only by recognizing the reality of higher orders of thought and purposive will. Man as a moral being is inexplicable unless the reality of the Universal Father is acknowledged.

"God is truly omnipotent, but he is not omnificent--he

does not personally do all that is done. . . .There is but one uncaused Cause in the whole universe. All other causes are derivatives of this one First Great Source and Center. And none of this philosophy does any violence to the free-willness of the myriads of the children of Deity scattered through [the Galaxy].

"Science is a quantitative experience, religion a qualitative experience, as regards man's life on earth. Science deals with phenomena; religion, with origins, values, and goals. To assign causes as an explanation of physical phenomena is to confess ignorance of ultimates and in the end only leads the scientist straight back to the first great cause--the Universal Father of Paradise. Urantia Book pp. 53, par. 1; 1299, par. 4-5; 2077, par 1.

"You may still complain about fear, but you nevertheless persist in making yourself fearful. I have already indicated that you cannot ask me to release you from fear. I know it does not exist, but you do not. If I intervened between your thoughts and their results, I would be tampering with a basic law of cause and effect; the most fundamental law there is. I would hardly help you if I depreciated the power of your own thinking. This would be in direct opposition to the purpose of this course. It is much more helpful to remind you that you do not guard your thoughts carefully enough. You may feel at this point it would take a miracle to enable you to do this, which is perfectly true. You are not used to miracle-minded thinking, but you can be trained to think that way. All miracle workers need that kind of training." ***Course in Miracles***, VII, Cause and Effect, p. 31.

REDEMPTION

Yahweh says: "Men failed to be Law-FULL by My Holy Law that gave Health and Prosperity; and so I set it out, that he must be redeemed by Blood. And as it turns out, it is the Blood of My Son Omega [known as the Christ, Yeshua, Jesus to some] that redeems willing mankind, those who consent to the Golden Rule, the piety, and charity and Justice."

And so it follows that those who love God's work and His Vision for the future live by what is Lawful and Harmless in His Sight: "Do unto others as we would have others do unto us" "Keep without spot from the world" "Alleviate the tribulation of orphans and widows." And yet this is not difficult, even if it is not EASE-y.

What Ever Happened to "Freedom"?

It is said: Real Freedom comes from within. And here is the reply I return: Freedom does NOT come >only< from within. ONLY the freedom to THINK comes from within--not the freedom to behave.

Christian "Pauline" theology teaches "Freedom FROM Law," which produces complacency and crimes between people that then need to be forgiven. Luther's Reformation and then Calvinism both reaffirmed the right of the individual to take law or leave it, which played out as sectarianism.

Never mind, that the Christ's teachings are undivided, incontrovertible, and incontestably good--just as He spoke them on the Mount. Effects Yeshua Ben Joseph created, manifested and produced in people were all GOOD. Just why it was, or is, that so-called "Christians" want to do something ELSE besides follow the Christ's words He spoke on the Mountain, I don't know.

The Golden Rule--"Do unto others as you would have them do unto you"--in real terms, however, results in a license for predatory behavior on the part of those who *DO NOT* buy into it. Gullible Christians are sitting ducks for anyone who understands there's more than one way to think about a problem.

Due to that fact--originally--early Christians gathered into communities, to protect each other and maintain peace-able interests. No longer. Christian communes are in danger that attempt to exist in permanent loopholes for the dispossessed, the outcast, the unemployable, the divergent thinker.

Remember Waco, Jim Jones and Heaven's Gate? That's what they want us to remember. They want us to forgo the Kingdom which meant grassroots, bottom-up Volunteer-ism-from-the-heart and embrace--instead--the New World Order which values top-down controls, vacant of awareness.

"An eye for an eye and a tooth for a tooth" is the thought that placing a LIMIT ON retribution (since anger takes an affront and multiplies it, ten times). The New World Order has no such compunctions; they plunder indiscriminately, men, women, children, houses, neighborhoods, regions, continents. The only person who is actually >free< today is one having no relationships, no roles, no place that attaches obligations, rules, procedures, policies or agendas.

To achieve freedom from rule-bound behavior, what's left is an empty shell to which random experiences attach--mostly impersonal. In my mind at least, that is a definition of Chaos--a situation someone would never want to return to, a walking-around prison situation.

While indentured slaves [workers] may achieve an inner mental freedom, they never act out nor achieve a competence in manifesting the good that they envision is possible. That is the aspect of freedom that is missing from modern life today. Due to predatory and parasitic practices of Corporatism, no fair-minded, even-handed, law-abiding person can confidently compete against legalized extortion and exploitation. They will eat him alive. Even the creative person is not free.

Most people are socialized and sociable--as children--until they are methodically de-programmed out of family-promoting behavior by UN-agenda-driven schools; and re-programmed into indifferent, mechanical behaviors : e.g.,

I'm SO SORRY you feel that way";

"I can only tell you what I'm allowed to say."

"What I can do for you ... is ..."

Video games and television exploit sitting in front of a screen and moving two fingers on their right hand. Players think of themselves as "free" because they can "blow away" the figures that appear in their foreground. Pitiful. What a curse -- dehumanizing people. I could not devise a more efficient way of turning spirit/souls into demonic one-track minds if I had set my mind to that very task.

There is no freedom--either--where limits and boundaries are confused, arbitrarily fabricated, confounded, over-ruled and over-complicated. Peace abides with recognizably law-full behavior, peace is manifest and attains an inner spiritual repose only when people agree, predation and parasitism must be discouraged by law.

Diversity is not bad: Deceit is bad.

393..Everybody wants to "do what's right" at some level.

383..What's profitable is "competence" and "skills."

373..What's prized is "belonging."

363..And what coheres everything is "what's true."

353..Protests show "Intention." They act out intentions.

343..What people accrue appears to be what they deserve,

336..yet other effects truly "get in the way."

639..What is true is what persists. Error always fails.

939.."Doing what is right" persists. Iniquity fails also.

949..Experiences people get must be acted on or missed out on.

959..but if they just get stuffed,

969..eventually the outcome is chaos, violence and woe.

979..So, let us concede that our test ...

989..is to convert what we are conveying to our children

990..from sacrificing their future to preserving it.

LAWS of GOD

Arise from His Observing Results, Effects & Outcomes.

One would expect that Holy Law from God would be sensible and Good, yet not constricting, wouldn't we?

01 02 03 04 -- What works best to sidestep predators is to share with those whom you trust and apply political action and pressure to those in whom trust is impossible.

06 31 07 32 -- Teach the teaching, that work attaches a person to real truths they can share profitably..

09 34 52 10 -- Endurance means, you get a turn at occasional opportunities and options to show your level of awareness and skill. Gains are possible only when you awaken some important and recognized need..

12 37 55 73 -- Self-sufficiency is what counts, not impossible hopes.

13 38 56 74 -- An investment in severals sets of tools provides adaptability that justifies a person's having to tolerate occasional work.

14 39 57 75 -- What usually comes up are ways to prompt people and do for them what they cannot or do not want to do for themselves..

15 40 58 76 -- People pushing their values on others run into a great deal of resistance; so, why not just acknowledge the Good in ALL but confront problems?.

16 41-59 77 -- When you cannot stand with a direction you are given, a simple, "No, that is outside my boundaries" will suffice. Anything more will foment an argument..

17 42 60 78 -- When one consents to a set of practices, you better be clear about the reality to which its adherents consent. Don't be a drummer if you hate noise..

18 43 61 79 -- What seems Good at the time is certainty; but what is actually True is seeing to it the afflicted are comforted and the comfortable are afflicted..

19 44 62 80 -- Nice thoughts do not substitute for the experience of knowing how to reckon, reason and judge..

20 45 63 81 -- What's most appropriate is to harmonizing present Good with a necessity to "get on with" problem-solving. There's nothing to get on with if it's all final and already in the Book..

21 46 64 82 -- One becomes aware of his/her own role as he or she composes the "stand" they must take on Good and Evil, initiatives being taken and possessions hoarded before the Universe and God..

22 47 65 83 -- A commitment to be fair is also a belief that every person at least deserves to exercise the ability to cope, to attain to options that succeed, to initiate actions reflecting some form(s) of competence..

23 48 66 84 -- What is essential for each one is getting and taking turns in community and functioning by composing, by themselves, the perspective they must portray to create Good for others, themselves and everyone..

24 49 67 85 -- What is fair is being mobile enough so that experience dictates one's path [not Rules]: Reality should be fun and contain surprises and adventures..

25 50 68 86 -- Promoting Goodness has more to do

with strengthening self-control and self-direction than it does serving any single function, ideology or master..

30 60 80 00 -- What works in time is what works out for Good for the greatest number..

29 59-79-99 -- Communities must sacrifice ~only~ what is wasteful and oppressive,

28 58-78 98 -- and convey only what is essential for a Free Spirit to know..

27 57 77 97 -- God YHVH prompts His favorites; but He helps all work for Just Law.

25 56 76 96 -- What is Justice? That each Soul get chances to act out values; to walk a walk..

25 55 75 95 -- What is most profitable & prophet-able is to prompt simplicity and economy..

24 54 74 94 -- What is fair is allowing people to consent to the experiences they get..

23 53 73 93 -- What's sufficient is for a soul to profit from life and strength, and to learn to count continuing attachments as lifestyle issues, not as preferences..

22 72 92 -- The one commitment we promote in everyone is responsiveness, to specify what is "good" and confront what is "harmful," and therefore inappropriate for our town.

21 51 71 91 -- Being aware of one's burdens before one speaks UP, one comes to realize--sooner--that what you said is what you have to deal WITH..

20 50 70 90 -- Send out your thoughts [pray] for help and strength when you cannot meet your commitments, so those observing you from the Subjective do not simply judge against you..

19 49 69 89 -- "Legal" thoughts, when experienced, yield true wisdom, and they essential convey prosperity. SO: To manifest Good, eschew harmful thoughts..

18 48 68 88 -- What's "right" is a spiritual certainty when you see it; therefore, any person [or process] that functions as "leader" must lead by harmonizing needs of divergent communities and populations..

17 47 67 87 -- When a person consents to a belief, they must also cope with the point-of-view that it actually represents..

16 46 66 86 -- A person standing in a role must compose the perspective by which it can, will and must function.

15 45 65 85 -- Every human must learn how to read and write, to accumulate wisdom [their own and others] and inspirations they get..

14 44 64 84 -- The way to actually mobilize people is to establish processes that certify moral, ethical and professional competence and direct people generally what is Right to do under ordinary, predictable circumstances..

13 43 63 83 -- Simply being open to taking one's turn [as turns arise] is coherent with the teaching [also] that "having competency really matters because you get your turn sooner.".

12 42 62 82 -- Dealing with "what is Fair" is a discipline in which being clear about measures, metes and bounds is fully understood at all levels--cognitive, physical and spiritual..

11 41 61 81 -- It is appropriate to thoughtfully direct one's personal feelings towards what is good, appro-

priate and safe for all..

31 30-65 66 -- Staying engaged is harder when one is subject to a lot of complaints.

32 29 64 67 -- In a true commitment, confronting each problems yields solutions and resolutions, so that one's continuing in a particular role is then facilitated and progressed..

33 28 63 68 -- But, when lies and tricks are at work, teaching what coheres to cause and effect never achieves any real competence, for the confusion inherent in deceit..

34 27 62 69 -- "Doing a discipline" means a person has to cope with its typical doctrinal choices, over time..

35 26 61 70 -- What is profitable is being able to respond with clarity and compose one's own statements, as needed, that evoke Good in other spirits, people and animals.

WHY DON'T PEOPLE COOPERATE TOGETHER ANYMORE?

They're scared, that's why. Sectarianism rules.

1. The US Govt already knows because of lawsuits filed, that fluoride aspartame, hydrogenated and trans fats, and chem-trails all cause widespread health problems. And yet they permit these chemicals to persistently be spread in the American environment.

2. It appears that corporatism and politics are turning toward genocide, and a "lifeboat mentality" exists in which only an effete elite are presumed to be able to survive.

3. In 2003, Nicholas Turse, doctoral candidate at the Center for the History & Ethics of Public Health in the Mailman School of Public Health, that says-- in part-- QUOTE--

"It's time for Americans to recognize that people across the globe are now, essentially, being used as experimental material -- the test subjects for weapons technologies"--UNQUOTE.

4. A verdict from the International Criminal Court rules that members of our Government are guilty of war crimes and genocide. So, what will become of the United States? Will our nation be plundered and partitioned?

5. The Waco incident, the WTC incident and the New Orleans flood all show that the Feds essentially test incendiaries on ordinary people--treating working and/or cooperating adults and children as test objects.

CONCLUSION.-- Terror is how TPTB drive home the message: "Cooperation is useless and foolish and dangerous, and we're going to make sure people know this." Notice how Elites are never touched by terror, only the people.

"Get your tax exemption and only give to "approved" charities" [whose work is known to be harmless to the system], is the message.

"DON'T go off and try to do anything 'new,'" is the message. "DON'T RESIST," is the message, "or else."

So, for peace-loving and reasonable people who want to survive the coming American holocaust, remember, we must do so unobtrusively--as Christians did in imperial Rome in catacombs, as Yankees did who hid and transported slaves, as Germans did who hid and transported Jews and others. We who must cooperate to survive must be secret.

IT TAKES COURAGE TO COOPERATE, SHARE, CARE

What would cause the Illuminati system to tumble like a house of cards?

ONE: If we the people would abandon evil and establish what is DECENT, LOCALLY. Yes, of course, people can band together with those they already trust, abandon banking and money system--as foolish as that may sound.

Stop using credit. Stop depositing money in banks, reduce the use of fuel, stop buying any under-the-counter recreational drugs [all products the cartel sells us]. Like Hispanics and aliens who are dispossessed, we must dispossess ourselves of the system itself.

Here is how we can do this. Remember in the 60s we brought down the Vietnam War, by "dropping out." We must do that again.

Replace credit cards with postal money orders for the time being, until local pawn shops and credit unions can be organized, to liquidate stuff into cash and to save the cash.

Use and establish pawn shops to liquidate hard goods and buy less-than-retail ALL THE TIME. Pawn shops and consignment shops and flea markets and yard sales must become our WalMart.

Organize food coops to cut the spiraling cost of groceries, and form the basis for negotiating with today's pawn shops for cash liquidation options that are fair, in well organized and ethically-run pawnshops and lawfully established credit unions. And that's going to take all the brains we've got.

GET OUT of the banking money system. GET OUT of the retail system. GET OUT of the labor system. Barter, swap, set up skills banks and baby-sitting cooperatives where parents trade-off supervising play time and nap time of children not their own.

Home or cooperatively school one's children, use free libraries, network on the Internet as long as it stands and works--who knows when TPTB will pull it down completely. After all, they're probably the ones funding hackers' bugs, so the Feds can slow the Truth down, now and then.

Let us understand: Globalism considers all forms of cooperation as seditious. To their hierarchical and bureaucratic minds, Rules are paramount, effects and outcomes, inconsequential. The old Soviet gulag has been resurrected as Globalism, with all its corruption, inertia and red-tape.

Let us remember: Every group annihilated by the US Govt has been a cooperative living situation, a community of sharing: Philadelphia MOVE, Ruby Ridge, Waco outright. And some suspect Jim Jones' movement and Heavens' Gate--had probably been, in fact, infiltrated by Government agents. I wouldn't be surprised; would you?

The point is being made that cooperative behavior is not only foolish--it's dangerous. We -- of sound mind and peaceful heart -- do not need to be intimidated by Feds' accusations that cooperation is the same as subversion.

If we are to survive to see God's Kingdom -- and it has become patently obvious to many of us that the US Govt has no further interest in our survival -- then hiding and covering our tracks becomes essential; and harmlessness is our way of being, in order to achieve these objectives.

Thus, let us organize and cooperate, just to exist, despite dogma, doctrine and belief that cooperation itself is both impossible and foolish. What have we to lose by doing something "new" [among ourselves], with the Holy Spirit is everything.

If and so long as we are law-abiding in civil terms, what business is it of anyone's what our thoughts are, or whether our hearts and souls belong to God?

Let's not look at anybody as an Enemy. That's "*stinkin' thinkin", to quote Alcoholics Anonymous*. What is real is, indifferent processes, procedures and policies set up to:

1. Consolidate everything.
2. Commercialize everything.
3. Classify everything.
4. Claim everything.
5. Control everything--legislate to benefit elites only--not supporting people who work and have families.

So, let us do a workaround this problem; let's remain law-abiding, as our Lord commanded us at Matthew chapter five.

I realize, in today's marketplace, foolishness is nearly a fatal mistake. The appearance is created that SHARING is foolish because --so the dogma goes-- every victim has a Govt source they can suck on. Well, that's not true. America has a large percentage of homeless citizens in the world, and one of the most corrupt governments on the planet.

http://www.pbs.org/moyers/moyersonamerica/capitol/index.html

Let us reestablish the foolish act of SHARING with those not of our own sectarian group, not of our own nationality, not of our own race -- of caring for material needs of those being crushed by the system -- unemployed and unemployable [but sane], anxious, the panic-stricken, the abandoned, the newly graduated, laid-off, the working single parent, the elderly person on a tiny pension, the veteran who never got his stuff back together--share with everybody the system despises, it is God who blesses our sacrifices.

Then we will regain our humanity in the face of great evil. Let us put to practice the Sermon on the Mount, one-on-one--never mind, churches and empty pontifications! Silent hand-wringing just to keep a 501(c)(3) tax-exempt status -- does not work for Justice. Let us make the Sermon on the Mount our Job Description.

After money crashes and the political system hemorrhages and fragments, God will deliver us from the problem of housing by redrawing national boundaries so we can live and not merely serve as monkey conduits for developers and rich land owners.

It takes Faith to know this. Following the Christ works for good. Let us abandon the practice of not-seeing Avoidance, abandon the use of shunning/ neglect, leave complacency behind and establish what is good once again.

Reject "US Against THEM"!

This is the mandate Jesus Christ gave us; and that is what we must follow if we are Christian. Follow Holy Law : that is the mandate Moses gave to the Jewish people if Judaism is your Faith, the Commandments of God administered in the Covenant of Grace, which is undeserved kindness toward the afflicted. It won't be easy or even simple, but what is our alternative? Adopt slavery? Starve? Prison? Detainment and gas chamber? chemtrail casualty? Plague victim?

May we reestablish Decency, Kindness and not Passivity or "not-see-ism" is the outcome.

"Let anyone thirsting ... take Life's water free" if need be. But donations make things happen. ... Haven't you ever said--"Let's DO something!!"

Do you realize, it's time to do some things for ourselves ??

Government has plundered and is plundering and pillaging people. We CAN help ourselves by helping each other, or we'll all suffer and perish.

Just think! Become aware!

How would your personally sharing what you no longer use or need, benefit someone else?

The Law of Ten benefits one's own community-as-a-whole-- how much more resilient that community becomes when people >share< what they no longer need.

Let's think about awareness and strengthening the bonds of families and community.

Here in the US, industry is largely moving out. YET-- Leading and facilitative and enterprising initiatives still require we trade with money.

Identify functions that can be met for nothing or very little, mostly by volunteers helping each other, by surplus donations and donations from readers like yourself. Create a :

* Foundation -- ENDOW or GRANT Land for a Campground and pet cemetery-- a place to go for the temporarily embarrassed working family;

* Secondary cash-cow -- Establish Consignment, Recycling and Refurbishing center for gathering and resharing cast-offs: cans, bottles, rags, crops, plastics and furniture to sift, sort, repackage --as Goodwill used to do--all volunteers, living in the campground rent-free;

* Tertiary services-- Coordinate a Skills desk to call or go to--where resident workers show up and share what they know; man the phone 24/7; provide maintenance, day-care, laundry, kitchen, library-help, outside day-labor and temp services for cash;

* Add-ons --Not multilevel marketing -- provide skill-based interests: cooking classes; a pawn shop to buy, sell and liquidate "stuff" and raise cash; dog-obedience-training [for home security], cooperative Libraries for books, media, tools and seeds, tutoring, and so forth.

What you GIVE comes back to you 10 times--Bad or GOOD.

By Contrast--Greed is the desire to **keep hold of more** than one's material needs-- acquiring and hoarding "extra stuff." Most of us have attics, garages and tool sheds full of extra stuff.

What if your extra stuff can become someone's lifeline in this time of the end, this Tribulation? Why not clear your decks and give somebody else a hand up?

WHY NOT give all your extra stuff away, ... so it can do somebody some good?

Would that change the world??

Let's look at it this way.

Giving somebody a chance to do something with A cast-off FREES BOTH the Giver and Receiver.

Freeing the Giver-- When you share from your abundance, you are freed three times:

* Sending money, bequeathing land, turning over an old usable car, truck, camper or trailer, you become truly free from the worry and hassle over ownership.

* When people know a donation will be used honorably, it feels good, to give--plain as that.

* In asking for donations, we provide you the chance and enable you to put the Law of Ten into operation in your own life--"What goes around, truly does come around." Give and get back Good.

Freeing the Receivers--

* Giving a chance to the unemployed and underemployed to associate together with leaders--not just a dole--and have a place and a reason to "be family."

* "Exploiting loose 'stuff' and making something useful out of it is better than acting out a dependency script.

* Using what free time we have to meet needs of those in deep lack, we develop skills in the process --

marketable, useful skills and learn the skill of cooperating.

WHY NOT give away Money, Land and unused stuff? And allow your gift investment to create a chance to put to work; have faith that Gifts will be returned in time, in many ways.

"It feels to me as if giving is an extension of Reason. Having my money, my time and resources speak for me is what I value and support. "

At the same time we all acknowledge the perversity of human life. I mean, What makes men chase women they have no intention of marrying? . . . The same urge that makes dogs chase cars they have no intention of driving. So, we stopped trying to guess intentions, and just take note what happens next. If it's good, that's fine; but if it's bad, well then, it's bad. We get to experience the bitter as well as the better.

HUMAN HISTORY GOES BACK, BACK, BACK

As we all now know, the history of mankind does not begin at Genesis, obviously. A great deal of knowledge of what had existed long ago was was destroyed in the fire that burned the Library at Alexandria, Egypt. What we have left in our Bible is a brief summary; and it only goes back about 6000 years.

I realize there are Christians who insist this planet is only 6000 years young; and I'll just leave that argument right there on the table, untouched. We have hard physical evidence of much more.

There is a critical path thread, from the beginnings of recorded artifacts until now, that a "fight-to-the-death" over methodology for evolving the humans on this planet has been going on since the times of the Sumerians, the Egyptians, the Greeks, the Romans, the Celts. This battle of methodologies is personified in a contest between Yahweh, God of Creation and Enki/ Satan/ Lucifer, the God of "this world," by whose influence men choose the Dark Side.

Even now Mystery religions are paternalistic and coercive top-down hierarchies that continue to incite loyalties of Rich elites, even in America, utilized as props to keep society off-balance, officially cull and eliminate minorities, especially devout Christians who follow Jesus' quite revolutionary method.

Jesus dropped out of His Society because that Society had forgotten who they were:
In Covenant with God, in relationship to Holy Law.

World War One financed by the City of London and the Federal Reserve --both built on Rothschild's model after the sinking of the Titanic-- eliminated all opposition to Wilson's fiat-money plan.

War War I trounced all King George V's cousins, his aim, to seek a more imperial and global role and refuse to acknowledge the outrage of his cousin, Tsar Nicholas, at personal slights based in an Illuminati plan to consolidate all sovereignty under one globe rule, and eliminate everyone else.

As a result, the Tsar's reign was subject to manipulations of disaffected Zionists and Continental bankers. And so a feud in the British Royal Family between Royal Globalists and the Tsar resulted in toppling the tsar and his family; and it spilled over into war and profit-taking (over the price of gold) against the German half of the Royal family by the Bank of England. Yes, World War I and all its bloodshed was a family fight of the Windsors against each other. History books don't tell us this.

World War II was a continuation of WWI financial strains; but by then, Zionist Bankers' and Elites' conspiracies to force single planetary rule (to create a Zionist secular state after the manner of Annunaki/ Theosophical/ "ascendant hierarchy,") were well under way "in back rooms by the Rich.

In-fighting, called Hegelian Dialectics, set viewpoint- against-viewpoint and culture-against-culture using movies and media, to generate corporate profits and maintain distractions from real workings of banks, currencies and mounting debt.

Beginning in the 1940's the appearance of UFOs and the assimilation of Not-See Germans into the American scientific communities (*Operation Paper Clip*) deeply emboldened Washington to spread Secrecy and the method of communism:

The end justifies the means, is their method

. By embracing Fascist abusive methods, the defeated Germans sent their Not-See human experimenters, psych-op specialists and pharmacologists and sent them off to America so the Annunaki paradigm [using people as objects of research and genocide] was seeded to America. "Let's see what would happen if we try this," became the mantra of cynical and cruel scientists.

Double-Dealing As Official Policy, by Michael Salla is a report on US/ET Relations that documents America's negotiations with ET visitors in 1954 pre-empted by David Rockefeller (who established Annunaki Foundations and charities pushing for genocide and slavery) negotiations in a spirit of duplicity and double-dealing in talks surrounding the *Greada Treaty* (and later, the *Tao-Nine Treaty*) that Presidents Eisenhower signed (in 1954) and President George Bush Junior

(2006) ..

There is a power, a force behind the group of men organizing and redirecting change. It's an inter-dimensional reality. And just LOOKING AT its products, one realizes its origin. These ETs and their ideas are the Annunaki's, returning their attention toward our planet since around 1975; although their Mystery Religions' and "New Age" adherents have been here all along.

We may not be able to recover what we had when the final Bell rings on this Capitalist-Global system which is ruining this planet. Maybe that is not a bad thing. Maybe what we need are civil guidelines that are relationship- and communication-ORIENTED.

Maybe the real currency is language articulation and tactful speech. Maybe the labor that makes the most sense to human life is that which protects by keeping things clean, in order where they can be found, for the season in which they are utilized. And everything else is just "stuff." I hope this message serves the purpose of giving folks some new ideas.

In God's Grace and Good Hope

Shechaiyah, March 2016

Diversity UK/USA

A MODEL OF COMMUNITY for the 21st Century

CONSIDER : Let's see where we are. We are NOT, as the Qumran commu nity HAD to, passing hot and arid desert scapes. Ours is a different aeon, a different set of circumstances God has given us to contend with--cold and not heat--with deteriorating atmosphere and pollution.

Our children are our futures

CHERISH THE CHILDREN

LOVE--AS PHILOS--IS FROM GOD

737--Devote yourself to assessing behavior and loving the child.

747--Attain doctrines that make sense, not arbitrary Rules.

757--Favor your children by prompting them in the present, not by berating them for the past.

767--Learn to cope with each child's point-of-view that their Souls take.

777--Stimulate activities without exhausting their Spirits.

786--What needs to be Real is "How to Function in the World."

685--What must find Focus is promoting THEIR perspective.

584--What makes child-rearing so exhausting--it's their life.

483--Buy into whatever process creates Competence--nothing less.

382--Adopt whatever tools of the Spirit [education] you can GET.

281--Understand that Health is central to a sound mind,

181--and learn how to identify and promote Good Health in your child.

192--Think about the kind of Lifestyle that will promote THIS child.

202--Put your heads together, and think about the Child's Future.

212--Be aware of your child's dealings; and keep NO secrets either.

222--Let your commitment to the child become a mutual commitment.

232--It's okay to want to belong as a family, to your child's Life.

242--It's Fair to discipline your child, no matter at what age.

252--Always promote the response that says, "My folks love me."

262--Speak out of Clarity, not from Ego, Exhaustion or Despair.

272--Speak of what is Just, What is Fair, and what is Merciful.

282--Know your child's Spirit at every Age and Station.

293--Confront their lives as if they were your own--to gain Clarity.

303--Frame the relation between you and your child as a prototype that God gives all His children, to satisfy Grace.

* * * * *

We can pick and choose our experiences from the Table of Life Choices spread before us: we choose some and reject others.

Driving inland away from the sea past the first set of foot-hills, there is a plateau that juts up for about fifty miles north-to-south along the length of the broad valley floor as you drive inland toward the mountains. We're actually at an elevation of about 1800 feet on top of that plateau. And if you turn off at the correct side road, you will enter a hollow where the land is deeply forested and sparsely populated as the mountains are farther on, but close in and in a political no man's land (which is convenient for maintaining separation).

Diversity is a community -- as Qumran was -- living its values. That means, all the residents of the community operate from personal choice, and choices differ. Everybody acknowledges "that Of God" in everyone else. And three strains of spirituality operate side-by-side-- people who "Abide With Favor" (by Holy Law); those who live by "Simple Faith" (the Book), and people of honor who are a-theists and agnostics conforming to a form of honesty bounded by pacifism, vegetarianism and inner silence.

We all live together in peace. For our readers who do not believe in God, let our results, effects and outcomes be testimony to the integrity of our intentions and behavior.

Residents stay because they want to live this way for INNER reasons, and they are NOT simply following their own "Personal Preferences," but what is comfortable has a wide range of expression, even here.

Affiliation

Personal preferences do not control us. Remember, Moses was not asking the Israelites about their personal preferences. Nor did Jesus advocate that His disciples live by their personal preferences, although Jesus did give his apostles authority to determine how each community would settle its personal differences and set itself apart from the dominant societies of His day. Yet personal preferences among His followers varied, even as they operated by the Holy Spirit of Truth.

The fact that people who live here in Diversity are willing to bend on personal preferences means they are also willing to come to consensus about the meaning of each element of life here. This is odd, you say. What do you mean, they "come to consensus" on ... the meaning of things?

Cooperate as in a Private Condominium

This means we have different layers of participation -- Visitors, "plebes," law-full residents, spiritual guides, occasional members and former members.

It means we have layers of obedience : obedience to social customs, obedience to Law, and obedience to God, which is unconditional when it is present.

It means, every person who comes here has the potential to be a Bride of the Christ or a spiritual Adept or a monk or nun or devotee; but not everyone makes all the choices and operates from the selflessness that makes becoming a chaste Bride a do-able goal.

In fact, since most our members come here after they no longer can find work "in the world," very few weddings here are of young virgins; most are re-marriages and hand-fastings.

Since it's a person's associates and relations that define a person in community, how the choice is made to marry is central to one's decision for a life purpose. Careless marriages occur among our visitors; persistent marriages occur among those who maintain God's Law as Holy; but mere hand-fasting gives way to an eternal coupling when two virgins who have never touched nor been intimate, kiss for the very first time at their own wedding.

Chastity

People who come to us, pay us money and take their chances to be here. But if they want to stay, then they prepare the way for their own children to live as eternal sons of God.

Generally, it takes two or three generations for a visitor's commitment to "behave" to be fulfilled as grand-children or great-grand-children who are chaste, truth-telling and courageous in their devotion to principle.

For reverent atheists and agnostics, I can only say, "The CAUSE must be sufficient to produce any effect. Whatever--or Whoever--permits humanity and ourselves to exist also indulges a large number of other life forms. God loves all Life forms. We enjoy the freedom that comes by day-to-day communion with Nature with animals and with each other--one and all.

What Diversity means is, each and every act, bid, and motion has meaning here because we choose to have it so. We chose to impute honor to simple work, to impute strength to pacifism, to impute integrity to different strands of behavior. But we also chose to specify all these choices among ourselves, so a culture emerges here in which every "thing" and every "thought" counts for something.

Modesty

The way people dress has meaning; the times they work and don't work are known and understood and have meaning. What is visible or not visible has meaning. What is FREE or not free has meaning. Who is a resident or not has a commonly-understood set of criteria.

What is done or not done on the sabbath is commonly

understood. How to deal with trash and refuse has a commonly understood meaning, just as dealing with language has a commonly understood meaning around what nouns and verbs DO.

The culture is taught from the ground UP, so there are few opportunities for REAL ignorance or controversy. This place practices Peace. People who find they don't want to do this, simply leave.

We recycle!

When we adopted a lifestyle devoted to commonalities, we remind themselves, each resident has made a conscious choice to participate. Most Diversity residents come from different places, perspectives and ideologies, and we have all 'been to town.' Life in Diversity is full, and we're permitted to be more different than alike.

It's accepted that problems will arise; and there are processes to deal with what arises. But we are all invested in the spiritual life, the inner life in one form or another. That is our common experience. Whether we acknowledge "God" or not, we acknowledge the benign intentions that "religions" have always purveyed as "coming from God."

Our way of life permits people to attach and detach, come and go seamlessly as their commitment to God and community ebbs and flows. What is constant however is, life here is harmless, economical, simple, and very, rich. It would take centuries for a resident to infer--let alone master--all the subtleties of life with which we abide that can be articulated here. The only real issue is whether an individual is willing to give up preferences to adopt a peaceful system.

Rational as it all may be to "consensus of the body," everyday living in Diversity still cannot please everybody who tries to live it, because we work at being an "ordered flock" yet keep very individual inner lives and personalities.

We will allude to the seamlessness of life in Diversity from time to time, and by seamlessness what we mean is that you will not observe anybody EVER telling anybody else what to do. All actions, choices, and tasks are voluntary by individuals who are simply responding to whatever is arising.

There are NO RULES to point at, only Values spoken. There are no signs to "Keep Off The Grass," or "No Parking," or "Don't Stick Your Gum To the Underside of the Table." Life is lived here so that what is appropriate is what is obvious to everyone. Those who choose to follow what is appropriate, stay. Those who have a Will to do something else, are facilitated to leave.

At the same time we all acknowledge the perversity of human life. I mean, What makes men chase women they have no intention of marrying? . . . The same urge that makes dogs chase cars they have no intention of driving. So, we stopped trying to guess intentions, and just take note what happens next. If it's good, that's fine; but if it's bad, well, it's bad. So, stop it!

Enter here

Driving north and approaching Diversity from the north-east, on your right there is a long hedgerow forming a boundary between the Village and your car on the high-way. The hedgerow serves the function of keeping trained and untrained geese and small children off the road. When you look into the Village Drive on your right, you see a neat, gravel road narrowing significantly to just six feet wide, and the road is one way--leading off north but curving to the west.

You will not be able to park inside the village; so why not find us a space over here (pointing across the road) where the gravel parking area is. We'd better lock it up.

There's a loo here on the parking lot, and a few produce stalls from May until October, and the jitney will pick us up from here.

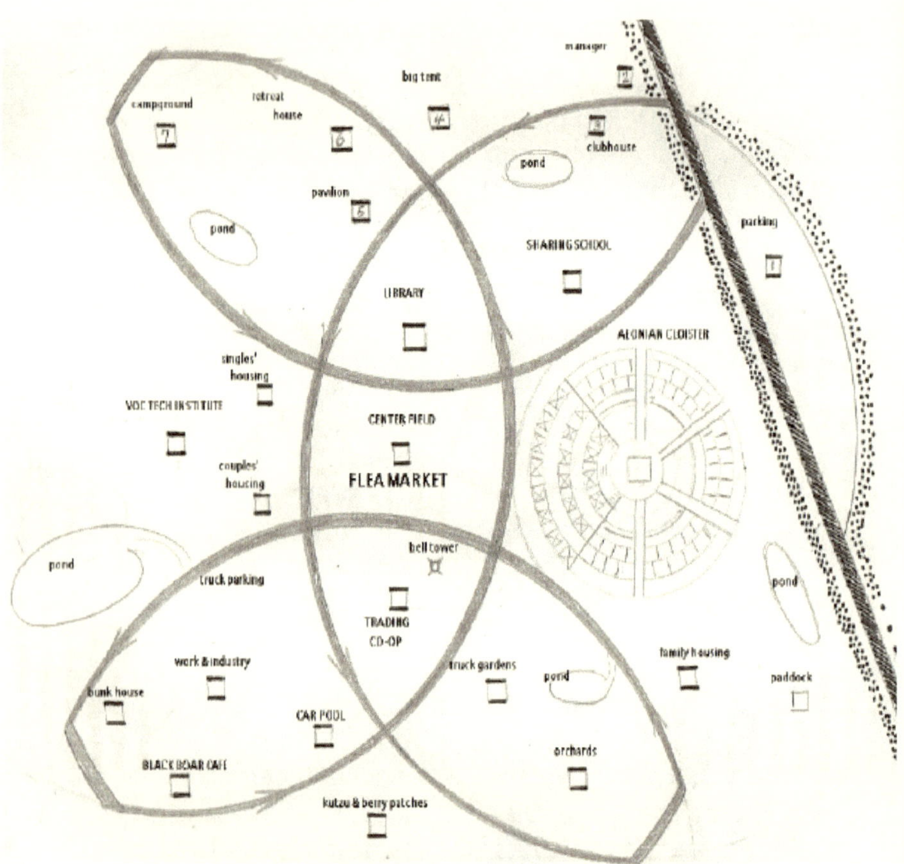

Stop by

On this parking lot a shaded produce stand is all we have so far; but we hope in the near future to generate more cash for taxes and other expenses by building a small pavilion here and an enclosed "mall" fashioned out of a simple warehouse with individual stalls.

Some possible businesses that might work out for us would be a crafts & consignment shop, a pawn broker, a snack shop, a gas pump and garden shop for local herbs and flowers.

While we're walking over to the Manager's office, let me tell you why I buy in to this whole scene. I've really gotten a lot out of the disciplines that come with living here. One of the benefits of the practices of daily journal-writing and weekly group problem-solving sessions is, we live our wisdom.

Whatever I discover during my workweek that AFFECTS anybody, I bring to the attention of the group. As a result, the town has developed stock remedies for many problems that we all can apply, and I feel as if I have some say in what's going on here.

For example, included in our knowledge of public health is how to avoid arthritis, constipation, foot fungi, dark age spots, mental confusion, circulatory problems, STDs and flu and colds. We address such problems and nip them in the bud. Nobody prefers a macrobiotic diet; but that's what we have.

Nobody prefers sweat lodges, shoveling dirt or limits on chocolate; but that's what we do so we don't have the outcomes we don't want. A resident who balks on any point of health will move out just as soon as they come down with the symptoms of the problem we agreed we would act to prevent. They feel guilty, so they leave. We're not free to be unhealthy, indecent or unwholesome--not here and not on purpose. Passive resistance doesn't work out.

Cherish children

Due to close proximity of our Village to technology outside, we avoid working for or with any business that does not adhere to a strict policy of utilizing renewable resources.

While it is true, some Christians work wherever else they want in addition to their work hours here to and buy whatever they want to have, the Village is organized the way our Village is organized; and "working to obtain stuff" is not part of Village philosophy.

Those who insist on working outside, also live outside as associate members. We are harsh in this respect. And looking at long-term goals, we accept that all experiences leading to Peace-on-earth are not easy nor simple, nor do they always feel good. Pretending to be happy is not our practice. We bear with lack, with disability, with abandonment, with suffering newcomers, orphans and the deserted.

We deal with death all the time. We bear with hard physical labor, plain food and devotion to duty, not unlike soldiers.

We are separated from the world, and it's a choice we all made, to give it up for something better.

Follow

Diversity Village takes up 1.5 by 2 miles, approximately 1,000 acres in the middle hollow between two hills. That is the minimum size that will self-support a community such as we enjoy, just over 200 souls. It is half forest on the high ground half meadows along the creek with shade trees and fruit trees planted, one grassy Center field, and only one large cultivated field because most vegetables and flowers are grown in containers under glass in the greenhouses.

You'll see glass pyramids popping up here and there. The village path is shaped like a clover within the its square boundary. The shape of Village Drive is the template for peoples' movements, and it was imposed on the land as forcefully as any Federalists, Imperialist or industrial manager might have directed.

The town path was bulldozed into its perfect shape, over hills, straight over culverts and streams and eked into hillsides because what the Village wanted was a command of distance and time.

The people knew they would have to take the time to adapt the land, its seasonal water-drainage needs and animals' normal cycles of migration to heal the road's intrusion. But that's okay because we have all the time in the galaxy to DO this.

All cars are parked outside the Village because there is only one road wide enough to support motor traffic. But don't worry; we can skip this bus stop on the parking lot and just walk into the Village to the manager's house on the right and pick up a jitney when it's heading east.

Oh, wait a minute. It's Saturday, isn't it? Well, we'll have to walk, today. When you can see geese on a pond through the trees, you're at the bus stop. Here's the bench.

A jitney will take us everywhere everyday (except Saturday), so cars are not needed nor wanted on the narrow Village trail loops.

We'll be starting out on the east Loop. You wonder how we truck supplies in? We don't need or have to buy "supplies." We live with what we grow and make. Only at Festival times do we truck anything in at all. But today's Saturday, so let's just follow the Jitney's path today around a couple of loops so you can see everything. Just two loops around, and you've seen it all--uh--twice!

Manager's Home

The Managers house is being built to your right, and her front door will face out to the road. Across the street, the Clubhouse is under construction.

Primarily the senior set come here and their primary interest appears to be Bingo; but they invite young friends and great grandkids also. We placed the clubhouse here because it is a disability-friendly building that serves our Visitors also right here at the entrance.

It's important that the public realize who we are and that the first impression should be consistent with reality when visitors first arrive. This is why we have placed the modest apartment of our Manager adjacent to a jitney-stop and at the entrance. This home is 900 square feet (approximately 30 by 30) and sits closest to the highway, visually fairly exposed, its glazed pyramid greenhouse a prominent sign to outsiders.

This is as good as it gets here. There is no home larger or more elaborate than this one. This is our model home, and it is quite modest by ordinary standards.

Willing volunteer Gardeners come in and care for the Manager's greenhouse plants every day, just as the Clubhouse is built and will be cared for and maintained by volunteers also.

When anyone has a question or problem, s/he must ring Mary's doorbell and be admitted. Ringing of the bell can be heard far enough from the house itself that, if s/he is not quite at home, Mary can hurry back from other duties to respond to a Visitor.

Sometimes it may take a while for her to return, but there's always a quiet bench space for sitting down and thinking things over, a cup of coffee at the Clubhouse, or if there's an emergency, one should proceed directly to the red door at the clinic across the street to your left. This is where the Med Unit is already waiting.

Clubhouse

There's a bus stop out front of the Manager's Residence for anyone who needs to come here to complain about something; and of course, the brand new Clubhouse is too, across the street, so Elders get first crack at the Manager's ear.

Also, because it's important that those of us who are sober and careful can preserve our home from sodden drunkenness and/or people flipped out on drugs, we have rigorous methods for dealing with these problems that sequester offenders out of sight.

Since we don't tell each other what we can or cannot do, anybody that goes on a spree is simply led, directed or carried to a hut down on our southern flank until they return to their senses. No muss, no fuss, no argument. When they sober up, they find themselves infested with fleas, mosquitoes, ants, poison ivy and black snakes. That generally prevents a recurrence.

After dark until 2am this area is patrolled by high school Elders from Voc Tech Institute--the High School--who have mastered martial arts and have qualified in tandem-animal training to become certificated for guard duty.

Their job is to promenade (walk) the dog-pig team around their neighborhood every so often and notice who's present. We don't want to run into a team at night. They deliver anyone they find in an inebriated state down to an empty hut on the southern flank. Believe me, no harm comes to them, just some discomfort. A dog-pig-goose team can makes a lot of noise and ruckus if they don't recognize you.

Between 2am and dawn adult maintenance men and cleaning crews alternate patrols with regular duties. Since we are not an armed community, we must all be vigilant to notice and report strangers and intruders so their needs can be responded to promptly and appropriately -- usually a drink of water, food or first aid -- or a hut shelter--is all they're looking for or need.

In this immediate area we're going to see the Clinic with the Red Door to your left.

Medical Facilities & Staff

The Clinic.--From here you can see a red door of the Clinic, with RED-painted door for visibility from the path. It contains an examination room, testing lab, all-purpose Emergency Room with four beds and working area for dispatchers who work 24/7 in four-to-five-hour shifts. That means a total of 16 people work 63 full-time regular shifts to respond to emergencies. All trained as EMTs, their job is to triage--determine the severity of the problem--and call in medical staff or simply alleviate the problem themselves.

All first aid is a response to effects. Equipment and supplies are maintained to handle injury as well as problems of communicable and infectious "disease." There is place for everything and everything must be kept in its place. However, we do not expect stoicism; pain and suffering are met with kindness, not paperwork. A person in stress is offered hot tea and time to calm down. They can talk it out, cry it out, or even cry and holler it out, and that's okay.

Incoming calls are screened for priority and relayed immediately, and there is no paperwork because there is no insurance company to deal with. (Anybody who sues us because we didn't do all the paperwork will find that we have nothing to come after; we live by poverty and trust in ourselves and in each other. Any brother who sues another brother gets walking papers.)

First aid (EMT) techs handle bleeding cuts (short-term), fevers (short-term), injuries (short-term), high blood pressure, low blood pressure, angina, dizziness, earaches and stomachaches, flu, migraines, anxiety/panic and child-birth. There is so much information in the public domain about handling health problems with simple commonsense methods, we have no need nor desire to escalate to invasive or expensive strategies. But, naturally, anytime some-one arrives who is very ill, our doctor checks in.

Cumulative records are kept on everyone; and these are absolutely private and never leave the archives, just as journals are private and never leave the Library.

During the day a second dispatcher also serves as driver for the Med Unit. At night the Med Unit it garaged at the Central Skills Center so a security guard can drive first for a doctor who carries a beeper and then to the home of the affected member.

There is a roster of professional healers on-call who can reach this place in less than five minutes: family practitioner, midwife, acupuncturist and homeopath.

There are no professional medical offices because they all work from the clinic or travel to patients' homes and take tools with them in the van. If someone needs simple surgery or burn-dressing, they are brought to the Clinic because several people need to be in attendance; however, most first aid, risk assessment and preliminary treatments are done in the ambulance itself.

The way our Healers worked it out, one of them is always on-call and the others carry beepers. Dr. Cutchins' usual hobby is to work in the formal garden next to Elder Apartments, so he can just walk across the street to the Clinic.

Or a med tech will drive him to a patient so he has time to get his equipment ready in the back of the van. Dr. Cutchins is also responsible for testing our drinking water in the village pond every time it rains, to intervene in waterborne bacteria and/or chemical contamination. My own daughter Dayna is working through her education so she can become the official chiropractor for the village. Wow. That will be wonderful, when she accomplishes that.

Helping Parents

At the present time we only have one midwife--not a full-time OB-GYN--for women and mothers. This means there's a lot of pressure on Dr. Cutchins during the night, so he utilizes a team approach to birthing. Instead of simply birthing new babies himself, he is training and assisted by Katherine the midwife; and together they are apprenticing two more new midwives in the practical aspects of birthing : making risk assessments, keeping everything clean, keeping the mother relaxed and confident, and dealing constructively with pain.

Every year the Clinic delivers about twelve babies, most of them in fall and winter. Maternal deliveries are given great care and preparation. Each pregnant woman is observed, monitored, and coached by our Medical Staff; they are all available.

When she becomes uncomfortable in her pregnancy, she just leaves her family in the care of Sisters--Yeah, we have a lot of nuns here, especially older ones--and comes to stay at Heaven's Door. She spends her time completing the baby's Layette and assisting other pregnant woman until her time arrives.

Labor is spent and her baby comes in an isolated softly-lit room (with music playing) so she and the new baby can bond without any distractions for up to 72 hours of the baby's life. Often, husbands arrive in time to share in the birth as well, but every new mother is cared for until all traces of physical stress have subsided and her nursing skills are well-established--as long as three weeks or as short a stay as three hours for a busy, experienced mother.

Alan Cutchins, Dr. Cutchins youngest son, is now in Medical School; but there is some question about whether he will come back here to practice medicine with his father. I know this is true because Alan has refused to accept the Village's support to continue his education.

Gretchen Maybury, a homeopath, has small children and is home most of the time. She isn't trained to deal with truly acute care, but Cutchins calls her in whenever a chronic condition comes up, because he doesn't want to rely on prescription drugs--they're expensive and intrusive--yet, sometimes he has to.

Mai Ling is the part-time acupuncturist, and she deals with local anesthesia and chronic pain problems, or she refers people to a local chiropractor. She utilizes the Med Unit most because she needs the portable gurney to work from.

In summer, the staff deals mostly with over-exertion, broken bones injuries, falls, cuts and bites of our visitors and Guests. In the fall, babies. In the wintertime, the staff deals mostly with communicable diseases, falls and spills and problems associated with babies and birthing. Also, the elderly become more vulnerable in the winter.

We had a situation last fall when one of our teenagers, Molly Smith, died in ballet class--that made us reassess all EMT procedures. But the fact is, Doc got there in the usual five minutes and they worked on her for an hour to get her heart going again. She had no parents; we had accepted her when she was six from foster care; and we figure she had had scarlet fever and nobody knew. We're all very sad and sorry about losing her.

Communicable Diseases

In case of infectious illness, the medical staff goes to the patient's home and operates out of the Med Unit, so as not to spread the disease to the Clinic itself or to its residents at Heaven's Door.

The most important job the Clinic has is to screen our residents and potential residence for incipient infectious diseases. All new Residents and animals are tested for STDs, TB, HIV, ARC, and hepatitis. This is because we need to feel good and not be vulnerable to diseases. What's heartbreaking is to have to turn down adopting an orphan due to chronic disease that would endanger the village.

As soon as we meet an orphan, the natural urge is to want to love them. And they come to us unannounced during Festivals when parents just want to drop off an extra unwanted child. But we must hold back and check the child for infectious disease, or we're just buying trouble later.

Residents who become infected with communicable diseases--flu, colds, or even more serious ones like diphtheria and smallpox--are monitored, their fevers managed, brought electrolytes, hot garlic soup and agar jello, clean clothes and linens changed (and re-sterilized) every day so they don't need to go anywhere or infect anyone else.

The jitney staff do this work. And after illness is overcome, the sick family gets three days Grace to scrub their home clean and sanitize everything from top to bottom. If need be, their relatives are called in to help them do the job of disinfecting everything in the house. This practice and procedure applies to guests as well, who come down with infectious disease on our property. Those (in the future because we have none now) who test positive for AIDS or tuberculosis or leprosy are going to present us with special problems of isolation, contamination and care that's a whole step beyond what we are able to do now. But God will show us the way if need be.

You'll see our blue and white striped Big Top is next, to the right. Then I'll take you around behind the hedgerow that hides our campground and its bad weather retreat building. That doubles as a gym. And behind that is a campground for flea market vendors right next to their field of tents.

We provide tents; they provide crafts, skills and wares for Sunday flea markets. Then as we curve around to the left we'll follow the path and pass residences behind a berm to your right.

See, the berm is just a gentle slope with another hedgerow on top, a sight and sound barrier.

Adapting to Constant Change

The Big Tent & Retreat Building

Since physical life is temporal, Diversity at first adopted a temporal style of Architecture that only exists when it is needed. All public buildings except the Clubhouse next to the Highway began as tents, as the Retreat Building here did. Our buildings evolve.

A permanent structure may begin as a concrete basements or pads with a metal warehouse stacked with hay bales on the inside and then bermed outside is a serviceable--if not beautiful--shell. And as we are able to support costs of conventional construction, our community gathering places are evolving into enclosed dome-structures with adjoining greenhouses. We did and do this because we do not expect the atmosphere of this planet to recover anytime soon from current onslaughts of chemical and biological polluters. So we put up what works initially;

and then as we grow we can think about beautifying social functions.

Naturally, the first "public" buildings to become permanently enclosed and insulated were those which must keep things DRY: library, warehouse, business office, newspaper. school classrooms, meeting rooms, the Theater and church spaces--even dining areas--water-tight yet open on one side to garden-house atria. Nobody should need sweaters when clustered. We're all under glass. Even cluster paths are sometimes glassed over so children play in the sunshine even in bad weather.

Pavilion

This large raised (on concrete pad) Public Pavilion is a heavy capital investment. It's in use year-round--in the winter as a garage/ cistern system and in the summer it's part of our Festival backstage facility. The cistern attached means it has water for clean-up functions, so it can also be used for sorting harvests, rendering tallow, milling lumber. It can also serve as a large public Room in summer, away from bugs and distractions.

We are currently raising cash to finish installing this pavilion; and its placement will be (on the map--as if the center field is the middle of a clock) opposite the Big Tent at 10 o'clock in the NW loop, right in that triangle. Such an important outdoor public and community building must be carefully placed, especially when it's this large.

Our other platforms are 10'-to-40' decks adjoining elevated walkways where kudzu and low-down wildlife may intrude at anytime. You wondered why we have dogs at all our Pavilion music festivals? Now you know. We also have intrusions by "critters", and we don't kill critters, just chase them off.

Walking down our One Way path here--what you see--

other than the intrusion of the jitney trail, is little to view. Why? because we respond to the way land is taxed in this county according to its level of development; therefore, all development must be invisible as possible.

Cash flow does not exist here to support our abundant way of life PLUS exorbitant and extravagant waste of tax and interest dollars that exists on the outside. So our community appears more like a habitat than it does a conventional country town and all desirable amenities are hidden away out of plain sight behind berms and hedges.

What the tax assessor or a tourist sees when s/he comes here is a nature preserve, mostly. The fact that people actually live here generally comes as a surprise. The fact that there are no power hook-ups; just one formal one-acre garden; no lawns, no conventional street lights, no conventional telephone poles or satellite dishes (just the Village bell tower and cell phones), no concrete sidewalks (gravel paths everywhere), no professional police department, no county sewer, water or state services--all these omissions makes the Tax Assessor reluctant to put a high tax levy on our lands.

And this is the way we need life to work for us, because we do not work for money here. We only share with each other what God provides. He does not give us money.

The Creator of all--Jews, Christians, Sikhs, Muslims and the Nations--has always attended to cause-and-effect. Otherwise, how would the Creation evolve and develop into Diversity-with-Peace? Scriptures say God authorized Adam to steward this planet; Noah, to preserve human community; Abram, to record his descendants; Moses, to develop Holy Law; John the Baptist, to notice effects of "lawless Law"; and Jesus, to model what is Good in the midst of Evil.

All these steps in the Covenants between God and

human families were progressive. Likewise, we see no reason for God to abandon cause-and-effect. Effects are this Community's primary indicators and lead to what needs to be done, changed or abandoned. Notice, God's works are Good. Let us do likewise and create what is Good as a model for all humanity, whether sacred or profane.

Strategy

What is Essential here is generally invisible to the eye because it's either underground or camouflaged. This is our goal and ideal.

What brought us together initially was the common realization of a group of Internet forum participants that our planetary oxygen saturation has come under attack by chemical sprays and electro smog; sterile seeds are now being mutated commercially, developed and trademarked just for profit; and so we came to consensus and made a decision to build a village specifically for the purpose of survival. And we haven't messed around.

Survival isn't cheap. In ancient times, community efforts were more concerned with appearances than they were with functions. As a result, architecture was cold to the touch; water had to be carried long distances; and food was only grown in muddy fields. The ancients permitted squalor. Women had to walk long distances to draw water from a deep well or distant stream. We do not permit this.

We're not doing >that<. We have invested in time-and-distance relationships so our home lives do not deal with mud, sewage, predators, exposure to cold, lack of oxygen or polluted water. We have gone the distance to provide a safe environment; if this is not fancy enough to suit some people, that's okay too. They don't live here.

We mulch all our waste, out away from our habitations. We collect and keep our water clean and available to every housing cluster and public function. There are no lawns except Center Field; all green areas (except private gardens) are publicly maintained as nature preserves with little disturbance by foreign plants. We deal with mud, slope, briers, nettles and poison oak/ivy, snakes, fire ants, mosquitoes, cockroaches, flies, mice and rats as if they AND our grandmothers were walking every inch of the village--which they are. We believe Life is precious, more than finery or appearances.

All residents are here because they expressed not only the desire to cooperate but also the willingness to be responsible for an outcome. Thus, most residents here are gardeners and gardening is the prime survival skill we learn and teach, specifically greenhouse gardening. Fully a third of our number are full-time greenhouse gardeners and we will eventually all live in basement apartments underneath greenhouses that serve us. In response to oxygen deprivation that industry and chem-trails worldwide have spawned, we all enjoy oxygen-rich air when we live with our plants.

Welcome

Guest Quarters behind the Retreat building and Big Tent consist of a spacious campground and trailer park fenced away from animals. Guests and new residents always take up there first. If they

don't have a camper or tent, we send them down to the bunkhouse past the carpool or we teach them how to build a wikuom (wigwam) out of poles and canvas tarps.

Pre-literate Americans built wikuoms in the Maritime Provinces, grass shelters in Florida, adobe houses in the Southwest, Ti-pis (tepees) in the Great Plains and Long houses in the Great Lakes. Native Americans lived close to

Mother Earth. In harmony with their environments, they built shelters ideally suited to each landscape. Not until many generations after the arrival of Europeans did they give up their preferred home-styles. In fact, people still lived in the old dwellings up until the 1950's.

And so--When someone arrives here homeless, the first skill they must master is to build a shelter out of what they can find in the forest; and we help them do this so it is an effective way to shelter newbies from exposure. From then on they must learn to garden as we do, to remain with us. We don't give homeless wanderers an easy ride; so the only ones who choose stay are those who can keep to our ways. The others find reasons to leave and we make it easy for them to do so.

Permanent Governance

As you saw, the village trail consists of four Loops (N, S, E and W) and the main Street runs criss-crosses the exact center of town. One village official elected for alternating four-year terms also lives at the extremity of each Loop: the manager here at the East Loop, the treasurer at the North loop, and the secretary at the south loop. Administrators may come from any of the spiritual constituencies in the Village. The chaplain lives at the west loop near the bunkhouse and mortuary. The chaplain is chosen for life, whose primary belief system and practice is "That Of God in Everyone."

Each year residents elect ONE new Administrator and retire one; during the fourth year of each 4-year cycle, the village takes on building project that becomes the capstone of that particular committee's tenure. In the fourth year, a new cycle of elections occurs. Of the three new homes built in the Village that year, the community donates one new home for the currently-retiring administrator, and every adult in the community figures six days work each year to help complete this commitments to the sequence of leaders from one competent manager to the next.

My own experience with this system--because I work in the Skills Center with the Skills database--is that I plan on working one day a week in the Gardens from March through October, and I plan on working for one whole week in the spring doing my part in construction. And that's IT. I work about four hours a day on the computer all year long the rest of the time, and then I am free to go teach classes, take up painting, or do whatever else I want. This is not a bad deal for me. Sure, I still sleep in my camper (with my dog Buddy and Cockatoo "Charlie") but that is certainly no problem. Besides, Charlie gets to go play at the Aviary while I work and I walk Buddy twice a day when I go to the Vet Clinic and walk one of their patrol dogs. It's exercise, you know.

Back to the tour. The manager's house is accessible by everyone. S/he is elected every four years to reside in this house, oversee and coordinate all Village functions and constituencies. That means s/he works a 12-hour day for those four years. That's why we build a new garden-home for him/ her on retirement, on the election of a new manager and return of the manager emeritus to private life.

Hardware Library

This is the central culvert, and we adapted this (and our Bunkhouse) existing building on the property to our own uses and needs. The Hardware Library is one such; it used to be a country store. In it we have located the newspaper and hardware Library because we're right next to the manager's office, handy for busy Elders nearby and the

Clinic too.

Within the Renflow Hardware Library, a Jeweler and Consignment area are set up as a convenience for those who are practicing the discipline of emptying themselves of "stuff" in preparation for a move or Journey. Across the street to your left--it's hard to see it very well from here--but there's a stairway down to the jogging trail that follows the creek from this culvert to the pond at the south end of the Promenade. You'll see the waterfall later on. Vocational Technical Institute is right over there behind those trees. From here tools and supplies for both our schools are counted and managed.

Next, you're going to see the main Library's white rotunda at this north end of the Promenade. It's a white dome, so you can't miss it.

VocTech High School

From Renflow the Jitney circles past VocTech Institute on the right, built inside the top of a hill. With twelve small warehouses adjacent to a large frontage field, VocTech houses departments that teach agriculture, botany and perma-culture; geo-pyramid and bio-dome construction; nutrition and food science; sanitation and restaurant management; applied chemistry (water, fuels and free energy); wood-working; stone-cutting; forest management and firefighting; textiles and tailoring; veterinary care, animal husbandry and *kashrut* butchering; magnetism and electronics repair. All classes are focused on survival and are open to both men and woman over age 14. This is the only vocational school of its kind that we know of, anywhere. Yes, we call a person an adult when they reach puberty, as Jews do.

Elder students' schedule in Voch Tech differ markedly from those in the Outer World. Students come in to school at 10:30 and wander off to Lunch at 2:30. This means they must begin their apprenticeship by about 4 o'clock, and they don't get off work until 8 in the evening. Young women usually go right home to their families; but young men often get together after work, and they are encouraged to hang out at the library around the TV, to play cards and stand Security at Central Warehouse, or help the guys at Voc Tech complete a current project.

Many young men work in the Veterinary Department training and monitoring Sentinel dogs. At midnight, there is usually a fresh pot of coffee on at the Needs Center, so that's a good time to take Dogs out for a walk. We keep the kids up late; they help with Security.

Village Elders see it as good that young men are out and about when the rest of the village is preparing for rest, and every effort is made to commend and reward young men who take initiatives to head off problems they encounter in the dark of the night (when everyone else is tired and sleepy). This is a time when wisdom gives way and lets youth mind the safety of the Village, until the first bakers and drivers begin to arrive for the next day's work at 3 in the morning.

This is why junior and Elder boys don't need to get to school until after 10 in the morning, so they can catch at least 7 hours sleep. (NOTE: There is no home work for high schoolers to deal with. When they finish their journals, they are through until the next day, except for apprenticeship and security work.)

Students who live, learn and work here have overcome major obstacles and difficulties to attend these classes. Many of them are adopted orphans and abandoned children of single parents. The Village itself has struggled long and hard to gain equipment and expertise to teach hands-on apprentices. VocTech's graduates can pull their weight, technologically-speaking, anywhere in the world.

We consider a young person for VocTech who has been with us since the age five or six and who shows promise in truth-telling, honesty, fair play and diligence.

Three Departments are of special interest because they are cross- disciplinary :

MECHANIX

Auto Repair is an apprenticeship program. Auto dismantling/repair, metal working and machining are taught at the Carpool service bays and warehouse where all our village vehicles are kept. The motor pool is considered to be part of VocTech Institute; and it is run concurrently with and coordinated with Voc Tech and with Grounds.

We're generally short on tools and parts; so all resources are shared between and among all three groups of tasks. Generally, it's a labor unit coordinator who is kept busy swapping the more expensive tools back and forth among different projects and functions, and it is they who must report an accurate count of tools and materials back to Counting on the last day of the month if their guys are the ones who checked them out and also the ones who'll need them again next week. So they keep track of where things are floating around. Otherwise, we all run short. We're always short on tools, actually.

The Carpool

Auto repair works very closely with other labor units, because we are often short of instructors for our children and maintenance people in general.

Mechanics make good teachers because they all have to learn how to explain problems and fixes to each other. Some of our teachers are retired military NCO's, some come from inner-city schools; most simply gave up on the concept of warehousing school children that is the prevalent philosophy of public education nowadays. But it is labor union coordinators who really make a difference in the quality of VocTech's graduates, because they can intercede in work schedules and bring in skilled workers to fix a problem someplace or teach students a specific skill whenever outside mechanical work recedes enough to do so. That way they can fill everybody's work goals in the slow season and yet give really outstanding workers a opportunity to show their stuff to the kids and get working credit for it.

ANIMAL CARE

God gives us our animals--diverse as they are--to care and keep, much as we do our children. God said to Adam, "Have in subjection . . . the animals," and we not only take this seriously, we take it upon ourselves to teach others to be kind and realistic in the care of animals of all kind. Our community even harbors black snakes.

Animal Care & Husbandry (ACH) serves overlapping functions in the community : as hospital and clinic for mammals and birds, and the vet department assists in all animal birthing and initial socializing. All pregnant equines, canines, bovines, porcines and nesting birds are brought to the Vet Clinic for whelping. This is to ensure that our Sentinel Corps are socialized to their presence so none of our Sentinels unwittingly eat one of our other animals--although it has happened.

But our Vets' really hard and manly job is to cull animals too sick or dysfunctional to keep--feral cats, injured or hostile canines, sick wildlife. In this regard, we follow the practice and procedures of *kashrut* to minimize suffering. Often we can place a found dog as an Elder companion. What a sweetheart deal for both of them.

Shepherds (for sheep, llamas and goats), trainers of Sentinel corps, bird keepers (chickens, ducks, geese, guinea hens, pea fowl) and regular dog trainers all operate out of the Vet department at Voc Tech. Twelve full-time residents spend their whole working day (dawn to 9pm) caring for animals. They love it. They never stop.

We obtained three burros from a rescue farm without knowing what they were good for or if they were good for anything at all. We found out what they like to do and what they're good for is sled pullers. They love to pull things, so we let them. They hate being burdened with stuff on their backs, so it made more sense to build little bicycle-wheel carts for pulling stuff under load. Burros pull wagon-loads of hay, building materials, melons or pumpkins, kids, and lots of gravel.

Alpacas are not so delighted to be hitched up; but their personalities are quaint and the kids like to lead them around. Goats and deer are simply a challenge to keep confined and behind barriers. But they're good eating, and at times we get milk from them, for cheese. Milking is not regular enough for us to consider them a regular source of human food; so we give our kids soy milk most of the time, and we make cheese for everybody whenever dairy milk shows up, and we gather eggs for the bakery, first, and then see how many there are for breakfasts. Yes, the village as a whole comes before anyone individually, unless there's a problem. Then it's the other way around.

Another rescue animal we got is an adolescent female gorilla. She's about two years old now, and we made her a comfortable "loft" in the VetClinic. Not only does she appear to grasp human sign language, she is becoming trained--with the help of Border collies--to assist shepherds. A young male Gorilla is not easy to handle; before we permit Missy to mate, we're learning from former members of a local circus just what is involved in housing a 600-lb silver back We realize they like to feel in charge; this could be a problem.

The hope is a female gorilla will become helpers with our flocks. Since gorillas are vegetarian, Missy would have little interest in culling the herd for her own supper. If she can be trained to help manage sheep and alpacas bred for wool, then we can become a rescue sanctuary for these large "animals" who are almost too human to consider as animals.

We'll see about this. If gorillas are territorial, they'll get upset when we cull herds for meat and leather. Nobody wants an upset gorilla in their front yard.

Since the diet of the gorilla and our herds does not differ greatly, they always know the best places to graze the animals; whereas our human brothers don't pay as much attention to the quality of pasturage. As things are now, they tend to prefer to graze where we don't want them to graze, behind bermed housing clusters [where berries and orchards are] too close to human enterprise.

We're training two chimps we got from a rescue zoo to "help" feed, protect and manage our chickens, ducks and also to assist in the Aviary, especially when we need to catch a bird and just can't quite do so our human selves. So far, they're very good at driving us nuts and keeping us guessing.

SECURITY : The Sentinel Corps DETERS intrusions.

The Village has a coterie of dogs, pigs and large birds socialized together and trained to sound an alarm when someone shows up in an inappropriate place or at an inopportune time. The Corps is comprised of four large mutts, four gentle border collies, six potbelly pigs, a pair of chimps, one young female gorilla (so far), and a gaggle of (so far) twenty geese and peacocks and hens, all of which mingle freely and are trained to ignore each other when we rescued them from wherever they were chained, caged or separated from their clans. Extra geese are being raised for down collecting and winter feasting.

Alarm System

One dog and one porker are paired with a 2 month old gosling or pea hen when they are four weeks old, raised and socialized together for Sentinel duty. There is a team for each loop of the village and in the groundsmens' warehouses at night. Their names--Abbott & Costello, Bud & Jim, Sleepy & Dopey--are comical by choice, and students win the right to name our teams after silly but appropriate characters.

The Sentinel Corps--particularly dog-pig-goose teams--are trained to notice whether someone is without a hat and is carrying something. Generally, if that person is carrying a large stick, a gun, a child, or another animal, the team will sound alarm and/or run over and bring that person to a halt.

Because our Village is known to be Unarmed, we all take pride in the way our animals are trained to fetch, to stand down, to smell out, to notice and to make way. We promote dog training for all our teams and teens, and we sponsor an annual Companion Dog competition each spring on the athletic field (or in the Big Tent) with team trials and exercises.

Pigs bred and raised here are a hybrid cross of small potbellied pigs and they are herbivorous; whereas dogs constantly require an expensive meat diet, pigs eat what for humans is garbage. These are brought up together, trained to patrol on lead regularly and to recognize who belongs here and who doesn't. Pigs also patrol orchards during the spring and summer and they empty fields in the fall and winter. They can plow up a field better than a tractor can prior to winter mulching.

Aviary

The Aviary is across the path from the Library. Its primary objectives right now are to track, house and breed large carnivorous birds such as falcons to keep the rat and snake population at tolerable levels; to promote the health of domestic fowl; and to educate and socialize two baby hybrid macaws (who will live to be over a hundred). Harry Hines the Ornithologist is a Teacher, not considered a keeper. I hope you notice the photo of the Aviary below in the discussion of school curriculum elements.

Glass Fabrication

We are a small commune, yes, but we have an interest in glass fabrication due to the fact we're putting up a large number of solar greenhouses that must withstand hail, storms, freezing and heat expansion. The Solite glass we are utilizing is from Torstenson Company in Chicago, and it's very expensive to order "off the shelf." We also have available to us large quantities of free sand and recycled glass shards, so Bennie Thurmond the engineer is looking into what it would take for us to melt our own glass and fabricate our own window panes. We think, if that can be done in India and if it was done in the 18th century by cathedral builders, why can't we do it? We'll see.

Library

Because Libraries are so central to all we know and do--as musicians, artists and craftsmen, as teachers and managers--the Main Library is where we have placed most of our equities in "things." Here we house archives, periodicals, a video theater, sound studio, one complete classroom, a large meeting room under the hemispherical rotunda, public phones, an interior courtyard and reception room. This is the real center of activity, especially on weekends when coffee and cocoa are hot and a selection of Sunday papers (with the funnies) is here to browse through. And this is why we set up libraries at the high school and Sharing School, to keep kids out of our really exciting stuff. Naturally, prepaid phone-cards are available at the Needs Center for work, trade or cash.

Collaborating

Jack and Linda BBlavatsky are free-lance trainers formerly from a traveling circus. They're not keepers either although they assist by setting up role-models for us to follow with difficult animals. We are privileged to have Jack and Linda here because Jack hurt his back and could no longer travel so they moved their camper here alongside a larger Village trailer and they are given as much leeway as they desire to supervise training of all our animal friends.

Besides, we keep and maintain close contact with Circuses--both for reasons of animal training and whelping, so each year their friends and former associates come back here--with myriad skills that circus people bring to us--in return for nearly-free winter accommodations.

Coordinating Need & Work

Transactions in the Village are based on the concept of 'a fair day's work.' After watching people work for decades, Elders saw fit to standardize, in small measure, the amount of labor required to provide for a materially-simple, but spiritually-rich life in the Village.

What do people need to build a village? What do they need to do and have, to live? Even in an industrialized society, human needs are constant and simple.

Here is the list which the Needs Center uses to 'price' and organize people's choices around the use of their time in the Village.

Time itself is the operating currency in the village; and it is residents' willingness to use their time to promote others which builds Value into the Village itself.

The Village men never just build a house; they build a house for "somebody they love who happens to need a House." We know, three families each year are going to get their new house; and we all love each other. And our old campers will have to make do until our turn comes, for a house. And in the meantime, Gary keeps my camper fixed for me; and he helps me move it into the warehouse for the long cold season, and back out into the campground in springtime.

And I mend Gary's clothes, iron his shirts and make him his favorite dinner even though he could take them to the Co-op and eat there if he wanted to. We're family, that's all.

Women here never just knit a sweater, they knit a Friend a sweater for her commencement Birthday. The children never just baby-sit for money; they baby-sit for neighbors who will be having a pajama party or snipe hunt on the Solstice for them.

Children learn in school starting in the primary grades what efforts bring what kinds of rewards. For example, a horse is a large expensive animal. If a child wants to own a horse, s/he is made to realize the cost will be some adult-level efforts to carry the cost and expense of owning it. She may even drop in the Needs Pavilion and ask, 'How many days would I have to work to earn and keep a horse?' And she would be told, 'A plain quarter-horse costs us 2 to 3 weeks of a man's labor to buy and another 2 to 3 days a month of labor just to feed him.'

For a little girl, being able to promote and fulfill 2 to 3 weeks of a man's labor is a big job--not an impossible one. But clearly, she would have to be highly motivated to want to do so. Alternatively, in a money system, a child's knowing that a horse cost $900 says nothing about where that $900 is going to come from or how much work is involved in earning that amount of money.

Use of Literacy and Numeracy to promote cultural values is known since the civilization at Ur, where Abraham was schooled in cuneiform writing. But, in those days, the only individuals who were literate were priests and kings. Now we all practice the art of accumulating Data and Wisdom and parsing the difference between what is Wise and what is Foolish.

Covenants & Promises

Moses learned to read and write in the court of Pharaoh; and it was the practice of Aaron to read to the Israeli people because they had not already mastered reading and writing. Yet, one of the fundamental *mitzvot* of Jewish Law is that every king must write down two copies of the Law, as a copyist. The Law was read to the people, on a regular schedule, just as parts of the Law, the Prophets, the Epistles and the Gospels are read in the Christian Church today. So Promises are made by the Literate, as Legal Agreements without Lawyers..

It was not until the Middle Ages when Gutenberg printed Bibles for the masses that literacy became widespread. Yet, in monasteries where copyists work constantly to faithfully embellish Biblical manuscripts, the Benedictines utilized literacy to keep track of their inventories of goods, in the storehouse. They wrote down lists; and many monks and nuns practiced journaling, to promote their spiritual development.

In Fundamentalist churches today, members think nothing of practicing exegesis by the hour and by the word; yet, when it comes time to make pledges for the support of the congregation's activities, the ministers still must rely on spoken commitments in many cases. There seems to be a prejudice against keeping track of what members can and will do to support both the inner and outer reaches of the church.

Yet, as a matter of fact, in secular volunteer organizations, Benedictine monasteries and Jewish yeshivas, the practice of keeping track of practices -- metaphysics -- is accepted, and literacy is valued as a sharp tool for accountability among its members.Thus, I present here a choice : to go on faith and hope that your skills bank will operate fairly, or, here presented is a process for determining the reputation of each and every member in the group.

Take your pick. "If you wanna play, you gotta pay," is what usually works to establish a good outcome. And if you look at the precedents being set by serious communities, you will notice they keep account of their resources.

A second look at an individual's Promise and one might sense it is appropriate for some groups and not appropriate for others; that it is useful for a period of time of establishing a community's skills-base but that it is excessive if adopted over the long-term. People are just going to have to wade in and see how things work out. I'm not here to make any predictions for you; I'm just rather good at organizing and synthesizing concepts.

Precedent

As a matter of personal history, I was instrumental (in 1975) in getting Xerox Corporation to update their service documentation; I got Arlington County (1985) to restructure their student lunch program; and as a consultant I assisted the Innova Hospital System (1994) in the redefinition of their Mission Statement and patient goals around the outcomes that patients actually receive. Further, my education is in conflict and dispute analysis (M.A., 1993) and I practice my trade utilizing a form of philosophical phenomenology called by the professional label, "interactive management."

The Personal PROMISE feedback system will work to provide your group with coordination and assessment of volunteer efforts. Whether it will give you the outcomes, effects and results that your group wants to see, is another matter. I hope and pray you can put this tool to good use.

For those values and services that one can obtain and exchange without money and without imputing a monetary value, Write Your Own Currency.

NOTES about Giving Personal Promises or Currency:

If you give out more Promises than you can keep, your reputation for Promises will be discounted or have No Value.

If you give out fewer promises than you can keep, you miss Opportunities for Gain.

When Value Received is $tiny, the transaction has no tax Value to the Government.

What you should offer to give is what you HAVE to give; time, effort, or something that money buys that is excess to you.

In this system Time, Effort, and what Money buys all have the Same Value.

EXAMPLES of Gifting

* Give your wife, for her Birthday, a Walk each Sabbath afternoon for a Season.

* Give your children trips to places you know they want to go, that make it easy for you.

* Give your friends the help that you would give them anyway, so they can count on it.

* Give your mother-in-law the gift of time with your Children, that she can look forward to.

PERSONAL PROMISE **dated____________in response to________________'s *WISH*______________**

For Consideration Received, _________________________________[*what I got*] I promise to *perform* the following "unvalued" service: [*access, barter, bequest, coin, collateral, donation, event, favor, gift, privilege, right, service, stock, use or warrant*]

____

for Promissee__________________________at__________by next______________. (*seal*)

In this Promissory vehicle, the Holder ("Whoever TOOK this Promise *in trade or by transfer*") will contact Promissor to arrange service. Upon satisfactory service, the Holder acknowledges fulfillment of this Promise by subsequently filing "this paper"—*at community*--sealed with the stamped-mark, "Satisfied," filed in the name of the Promissor within 48 hours upon fulfillment (within the usual fourteen [14] days). In this way the Promissor promptly gets work credit; and if no fulfillment occurs at all or late, the cash cost of this favor becomes a debit on the community that underwrites its Members' WORD. In this chain of events, accountability is guaranteed.

X_______________|___________________|__________________Promissor [*Signature/Location/Date*]

________________|___________________|__________________Endorsements [*trades/transfers*]

________________|___________________|__________________Endorsements [*trades/transfers*]

SAFEKEEPING

A safe place for Notes and Promises is to inter-leaf pages of a Journal or Bible.

REDEMPTION

Just as one must plan how to pay off a mortgage, one must schedule one's Promises. So, there should never be a surprise Redemption.

If a Promise becomes Moot (for example, if you receive two identical Promises), that's an opportunity to hand one on as a Gift or Favor to another Holder, and just let one Promissory know, his service will be needed elsewhere. No biggie. Pass it on.

All Promises have Value, so then let the new recipient endorses the Promise, receives the service, and files the "satisfied" Promise with the skills coordinator, so each worker has a record of their good works.

Endorsing a Promise over to another also provides the Opportunity for a New Promise. For example, the new Recipient/Endorser is now freed to make a different Promise of his or her own, having freed up some time. One Promise does not devalue a previous or subsequent one; so Promises tacked on to Promises only means people are being Good to each other.

Let's play a game now. Make a list of all the people to whom you want to give Promises, as if that were a list of investments--which is what it is--relationships in which you are investing your time. This list can include family, friends, business associates, neighbors, acquaintances--anyone from whom you are already receiving attention or gifts of Time, Effort, or Value. Remember the guy who gave you a lift to the garage, your son's teacher, your pastor, the mailman.

If you are like most people, you can only afford to give about One Promise each week. Yet this devoted time is an investment that will reap the Power of Ten for you. By making, writing or typing your list, you have also expressed and spoken your goal. That is like uttering a pledge. This is good, to set out positive intentions toward other people. And Good is what you will reap, if you do not tire out.

More gifts.-- By stating good intentions one progresses in their understanding of how to manifest honor. Such a list will serve for usually a season in length--so save your lists from season-to-season and you can come check back on the progress you make, between what you invest and what comes back to you.

Indeed, this is a great reason to practice Journaling your Lists. And notice, when you coach soccer, you are giving a mentoring gift to each family, not merely an entertainment gift to people who might want to be watching soccer.

NEXT, make sufficient copies of the Promise form, which is a form of currency, for all the people on your list, this season. Now the fun part. Write in the experiences that your associates want to have that you can provide, and decide on the best week this season to perform your gift, presenting a Promise Form--nicely filled out, placed in an envelope and secured--it up to two weeks before you commit to actually doing whatever it is. Give it in private or witnessed, whatever marks the occasion as conveying honor and the desire to endow, good for good.

It takes about four fulfilled promises until you see you life begin to change. If you like the effects that fulfilled promises create in your Life, then continue to make and keep promises to people. After a few (about 7) years of making and fulfilling Promises, having learned how to articulate, speak and write to the function of EXCHANGING BLESSINGS, one is elevated to the Status of a Guest.

Guests Help Without Generating Promises, in Suble Ways

A Guest is someone who is invited to participate unconditionally, in the life of the Community. A Guest [in return for free lodging and meals] can make the following efforts for a period up to four hours:

* serve and clean up in the dining room;

* walk canines with patrols; help feed and tend animals at the Vet Center;

* play a game with children in their environment;

* serve as ticket-taker and go-fer for Festival booths;

* ride on the jitney as driver assistant and helper;

* help find a lost child, lost keys, lost package, lost parents;

* care for the needs of a handicapped or elderly resident;

* make popcorn or serve lemonade at a concession stand;

* assist a broken-down motorist to get his car to the Carpool;

* provide a cell phone at a specified location and duration

* teach, preach, mentor, amuse, assign, clarify, proclaim or arouse.

The Dance of Times and Roles

Every town has a rhythm to its work and play. This town decided to establish a town clock and bell tower to tell people what time it is. Bell-ringers also serve as bus-drivers for jitney service; and their time is very busy indeed, to keep things moving along in the village without appearing to intrude. Animals live by a dance of the seasons. Because there are many animals who share our Village with us, we tend to be dominated by their bio-rhythms, to a large extent. By observing Nature, we have seen that "right time," "right place" and "right relation" are principles by which a healthy eco-system operates.

We also note that animals are grouped in nature by specie; so we group ourselves in the village by personality archetype. Each person is responsible to identify his or her "right place" in the Village, and to bring his or her experience and expectations to bear on archetypal (labor) issues.

Support groups for each of the working archetypes function in the Village as labor units. In this way the village has legitimatized diversity occurring in the ways and times people are willing to work.

Labor units meet in meeting places one night a week, usually Mondays and Tuesdays, to address labor issues in the village. The jitney makes extra runs on those evenings to accommodate workers who live some distance from labor meetings.

It is the labor units who set limits on the amount of work their members can and will do. There are no managers or supervisors of people where they work. The ones doing the work are the ones who truly 'hold the reins' of governance.

And when labor issues become unruly and disordered, what that means is that the time has come to consider splitting off a new Village so that preferences will once again become submerged into necessities:

* Split one off to the North if Fairness to individuals seems to have been compromised and the Village appears impersonal;

* Split one off to the South if no one seems to be standing For Honesty anymore;

* Split one off to the East if Deceit has divided the ranks;

* Split one off to the West if people feel inhibited and stuck for no apparent reason.

Village Transportation

Go jitney!

The different jitneys we have run from dawn to dusk on a 12-mile circuit, on the hour except on Saturday when the crew is off-duty. The driver, either Sandy or George, always rings the village bell at Center Pavilion just before he starts and then again, when he completes the circuit. Ringing serves the purpose that people will know when to get ready to be picked up, and then they will be sure that he didn't have a problem on the way back. It's important, not only in case of mishap, but also because the driver carries bundles for us which are valuable.

When it's dark, guests are usually comfortable in their accommodations and residents who move about light their Way with portable lights. The Sentinel Corps of animals are permitted to roam the village square at night (since they operate by smell) to notice any of us who live there and must walk the pathways.

Their presence keeps locals and strangers off our paths at night, as a rule, at least, those who have any sense. You'd never be injured, but I can tell you that being surrounded by a dog/goose/pig team backing each other up is not fun for someone the animals don't already "know."

One jitney has a string of trailers hitched on for parcels and bags, laundry, recycling bins, milk deliveries, and it travels only about 15 mph, so it's easy to flag it down if you want to. The village owns 12 vehicles and keeps them in its carpool: 4 cars, 3 tractors, 2 large trucks, and 3 odd-sorted jitneys keep the service staff busy maintaining them all.

In case of an extreme emergency, all our Villagers could be transported away from the village utilizing only our 12 vehicles, but we have every hope and expectation such an action will never be necessary.

Two regular Jitneys alternate working days and maintenance days in the service bays, because each one covers about 120-150 miles a day (depending on the season and duration of daylight) driving things and people around town. When you think about it, 120-150 miles a day for the purpose of facilitating the lives of 53 families is a very economical use of transportation. The third jitney, the med unit, is only serviced once a month because it doesn't get used very much.

Why don't we give names to our places? Is that your question? Why don't we give fancy names to the Skills center, the Co-op, and so forth? Good question. I dunno. I guess, we made a decision to keep things simple; but I'll check into that for you.

Summer Residents

When folks show up here during the warm weather season, we find them shelter. Either they come in their own camper, with their own tent (that we place on a platform), or they quickly learn to build a wigwam. A family group can stay as long as they are working at "fitting in." This could be a day or a year. So long as they are hooked into working crews for a shift (3-5 hours) per day (each member), we're not going to mind feeding and clothing them, as necessary. They can make use of the clinic, bring merchandise to the flea market, consignment shop and gallery, and observe all resident meetings. But their voting, teaching, and residency privileges are held in abeyance until we know them for who and what they truly are.

New residents will try to make appearances. This is okay. We realize it takes a while for the appearances to become real. This is why they are immediately inrolled in the Promise Exchange Money system, so they learn to articulate their exchanges.

[By the way, persons showing up in *new* campers don't need us; they're "hooked in" to the system. Generally, people who want to be here limp in with campers at least ten years old; most are much older than that. It's an indicator, that's all. Lots of very prosperous people are also very frightened right now.]

Family homes built here--three per year for recognized residents--are based on the geo-pyramid concept with bermed fronts and lateral hedgerow/fences separating the house-plat into a "front yard" and "backyard." But, as things are now, most of us are still living in the campers, trailers and tents we arrived in. And when it's cold, we all move into the warehouse in assigned spaces and make good use of the spa, laundry and dining room facilities until we get a home of our own for all time.

Gatherings

This is why congregate space is so important, because campers are not built for day-to-day wear-and-tear. In winter, RVs and tents move into this warehouse we utilize also as a gym and foul weather festival space in the summer and fall, from June 21st on.

It's a gym April 21st until Oct 20th, and we keep it spatially empty for retreats from bad weather from October 20th until spring is well underway. Spring and summer, we can always revert the gym to bad-weather camping space, and this warehouse is never used for storing anything but people, and the floors are not wood; they're waxed and polished concrete.

New Permanent Residences

Small geo-homes--some multi-level--nestled into a hillside (some with greenhouses atop), are occupied by singles, couples, families and affinity groups, and one with a greenhouse roof space can yield six crops per year of fresh produce.

Every home is a Faraday cage; some produce their own oxygen and fresh food. Vegetables, greens, roots and tubers must obtain fundamentally reliable stores here to assure survival; this is why we advertise Retreats almost exclusively in magazines devoted to gardening and horticulture study Groups.

Each occupant of a permanent home gets 240 square feet to call his/her own personal space. A singles unit has a 29' base; a couple gets a 31' base; and a family of four, a 37'-sided square home with full basement/garage below and greenhouse atop and 2000 square feet of container-garden space.

It is expected that each family roof garden will grow not only the food for the family living there, but also have food to bring to the community table and to the produce stand out on the highway. When someone "outgrows" the house they won to live in, they qualify to trade up. Growth in family is rewarded, not discouraged.

Sufficiency

Our homes are SO small, most of us spend a great deal of our extra (non-working)time socializing in the Village Eateries, Library, Theater, chapels, Co-ops,Skill Center or Spa, or we're working out-of-doors. So our small homes--just a place to sleep and take care of intimate matters--are felt to be more than adequate trade-off for the freedom and mobility that exists here.

Covenants that are in place to operate this Retreat Center specify different classes of participation, based on the willingness of our visitors and hangers-on to accept responsibility. Occasional participants, newcomers, regular campers, home builders, residents, volunteers, contemplatives and esteemed volunteers accept varied levels of responsibility.

But once a family is acceptable and accepted into this Perpetual Land Trust, their Name belongs here, and being here is no longer a negotiable issue. This place becomes one's permanent mailing address, voter registration address, library card address, driver's license address, and billing address for private phones. And one's occupation becomes "Volunteer Associate in the Retreat Center" itself--if anybody asks.

This is home. Moving into a physical "new house" will occur when one's Name comes up in the lottery to receive the most recently-built home. The House Lottery comes up at our annual Miracle Show and Festival at the end of the building and harvest season, what would be All Saint's Day in the world, the end of October.

Perhaps you noticed as you drove up, the building that is set off from the road is a round cloister built by the contemplatives themselves as their home here. We call it, "Aeonian Cloister," because it too houses Adepts, Contemplatives, Nuns, Monks, Masters, and Followers of Diverse disciplines. They have their own rules, which are much more rigorous than our rules; and they do as they pretty much please. Thankfully, they contribute generously to our produce stands, serve as a priesthood for the people, minister and provide comfort and care for the sick and elderly among us.

They teach us what Renunciation entails as we observe men and women at the point in the process of life where Wisdom and Spirit are worth more than gold and treasures.

Amazing people. Our kids call them, "Jedi Knights."

For ordinary volunteering families, at the building rate of three houses per year accomplished by two full-time construction workers and three days labor each from the other 150 adults each year, it will take seventeen years to house all 53 NEW families in new permanent homes. (Sigh.)

Working four days a week on housing, the two top construction workers have 450 days of fully "adult-but-amateur" help, somewhat as Habitat for Humanity does, each year. So they each get an adult helper and a half, plus a student-apprentice or two from the high school every working day. That's not too bad.

Outside

Single family cluster homes are separated by covered walkways and atria; five small-family units are attached around a large sunken dome or glazed atrium to house two dozen adults and their growing children. We added a large platform as a feature we call a Pavilion deck to two such clusters.

Two of these are octagonal raised decks (10 and 40 feet in diameter) and those serve as temporary public rooms when a tent is installed; without the tent, they serve as a quiet place to meditate in full view of everything, but without bugs and pests that live near the ground. That's what we learned the hard way when we used to build underground atria and had to learn how to live with bugs. Now we put sun spaces up in the air, not down in the mud.

We endeavor to be reasonable and provide people with accommodations that are breathtakingly beautiful, though simple.

The square-home clusters in this area (without a central geo-dome) have a lateral (side) barrier--usually a hedgerow--that serves as barricade between front- and backyards. The rear yard may have a fruit tree (fresh or for jams & jellies), berry vines (for jams, jellies and sweet wine) or grape arbors (for red wine).

In winter a rear yard area can also serve as an enclosure for small grazing and wandering animals, sheep, goats, deer who happen by and domesticated rabbits.

Activities on wheels take place out front of each house along Village Road.

"Hanging out the wash" occurs in the greenhouse in winter and on elevated clotheslines in the backyard in summer. There are no electric clothes dryers here, nor swing sets (to duplicate what is at the park or the school); although parents have been known to put up an elaborate tree house for more daring offspring, especially if there are small animals in the backyard that leave droppings.

Where large animals congregate, we use a hedgerow on top of mounded berms, and these create a solid barrier, even for a goat (that can normally jump up and stand with all four feet on top of a fence post). But we design berms to be deer-proof; it will take a military tank to get over them. More important than this, they provide thermal mass that collect and retain heat for walkways.

A geo-dome can be surrounded by greenhouses with fenced side yards. One such large geo-dome serves as Aviary for Harry Hinton, resident ornithologist, who teaches classes for VTI. It's located on your right behind this mounded hill but not visible from this point on the path.

You have to know where to look for it because that cluster sits low to the ground at the same level as basement apartment-pyramids that abutt to it.

Beginning with residency in a tipi, camper or tent, each resident learns to adapt to our careful ways, or they move on. Diversity is not about unbounded "Freedom" to do as one pleases or prefers. Hunting is unknown here except during very specific times and dates; no one is free to toss trash, serve bad food, act carelessly, speak out of turn or with contempt, ridicule others, make messes or vandalize property, embarrass neighbors, harm animals, abuse space, role or time. We are a care-full, care-taking community because this is a Retreat Center for others.

When it snows we wear snow shoes outside so as not to trample soft ground; we protect everything from being unduly disturbed. We have to cut across a field, so we are mindful of effects we make in wildflowers, across thorn barriers, through poison oak stands (on the extremities of the property), near large animals, whether we are wheeling a cart or carrying a child.

Community Design.--Village Center

The only vehicles that can make their way down here are bikes and carts on walking paths and large trucks that come in the entrance to the village, coming around the cloverleaf, making a left turn here at a particular driveway in front of the Co-op and unloading from that driveway; and then turning left again, bypassing all residential areas except Elder Square, turning right at the Exit intersection and they're back at the Highway 692.

This means, children at Sharing School must cross a street where trucks are permitted, so they are shown how to do so safely, going to Center Field for exercise.

Trucks show up anytime any day; we put no restrictions on drivers' schedules; but if the driver wants to eat, he has to leave his truck at the loading dock and walk over to the Co-op or the Black Boar Cafe, where meat, beer and wine are served. There are also pool tables, games, showers and a bunk house if he opts to pay cash and stay the night. It'll cost him--food, shower, games, bunkhouse and breakfast--about fifteen dollars in cash, barter, trade or volunteer time for a 24-hour stay. We'll work something out for any driver who's disorderly and in no condition to continue his route.

Who and What We Are

Constituencies here comprise four Service Areas, fourteen Labor Units, a Clinic, three Churches, a Public Clubhouse, the Co-op in which 'Counting, Skills Counter, Groundskeepers, Produce are kept; one barn, scattered passive magnetic power stations, Voch Tech, Sharing School Co-op, Library & Chaplin Theater, Carpool & Jitney, and the Black Boar Restaurant. At any given Manager's meeting, neighbors decide by consensus just "what needs to happen next" out of option goals they generated in previous winter retreats as adjusted by current conditions.

The Promenade

With Center Field to our left, you the Co-Op from here. This is where we'll have lunch. The Food Co-op operates in the Big Tent this time of year because we're in Festival time and the Co-Op itself is buzzing with the harvest. During really cold weather though, we share supper in the Co-Op building because it's permanent, well-insulated, and there are fewer of us to cook for. So they use the Tent over by the Pavilion, for service needs back at the Campground & Pavilion.

Underneath Center Field is warehouse storage. It's located here because most damage and trash that shows up occurs in the Promenade area, so all that is hidden under Center Field itself. Tools, tents, and out-of-season equipment are kept and repaired there.

The Co-Op

A triangle-shaped city block, the Co-op sits kitty-corner from the south work area on the left and truck gardens on the right. The Needs & Skills Room is in the Co-op year-round. From this central coordinating point, everybody (permanent and temporary) makes work arrangements, gets Meal Passes, and receives feedback about greater options based on current Skills and sweat equity goals each person is working to attain to achieve permanent roles and resident status.

The Big (blue stripe) Tent [that we saw when we entered the Village pathway] is raised at the Co-Op in March until the end of June for school competitions and stays up until October when all food gathering is completed for the season. After that, all social activities occur in the Co-op, in private homes, in the three churches that support and sponsor building projects, in the Libraries and schools.

During winter public meals are reduced, of course, because we have fewer people wandering around. School kids eat breakfast at school; and then after school they come here for lunch, and working adults come after their work shift for their main meal of the day. But dinner is usually a small snack of soup or stew and bread at home in the evening. The Co-op just serves one meal a day during the winter time when everybody comes in at once around 2pm.

Regular Service

The Co-op contains a bakery oven and facilities for making soy-milk, soy-cheese (tofu), and bread in very large quantities all year long. Twelve people (temps and permanent) work here every day to meet the needs of all the people in the Village. Basic commodities are sent out daily (with vegetables) on the jitney to homes in the village as well as to campers in the campground who request this service. Given a day's supply of fresh bread, a salad, soy-milk or cow's milk and a tureen of soup or chili, it doesn't take a lot of work for someone to put together a simple evening meal for a family.

Meal service is part of the deal for residents, but campers pay cash for a take-out dinner at the Big Tent when it's up. At 2005 prices, a dinner costs $10 for a family of five--to pay for the food itself. All labor is free.

The Big Top Tent (kitchen, serving and produce-selling tent) this time of year is back there where we came in the Entrance at Village Drive intersection up front. But when flea markets and festivals are held, and during summertime, when kitchen staff need immediate access to fresh produce for guests coming to dine with us, the Tent is out HERE. It's a building we move around twice a year. It's a store and restaurant all summer long.

If someone wants a meat meal, they are referred to the Black Boar Cafe out by the Car Pool, where meat meals are available for non-vegetarians Monday through Saturday; and what they charge in cash is very reasonable, about five bucks for a lunch or supper with meat.

Ride Sally Ride

Also in Big Tent temporary displays, we place vendors and displays of necessities that we offer residents as part of their "perks" and that we sell to visitors for cash or trade during Festivals.

Some accommodations can be opened up to visitors in the summer and fall if we have enough help : the Spa and beauty salon, barber, laundromat, kiddie corral and herb shop, when there are enough people to man them and enough interest exists in those services.

So, during the summer we have two focal points--not just the Co-op itself at this end of the Promenade, but also the Pavilion at the other end. Sometimes vendors line the Promenade in between also and this means "stuff" is constantly moving back and forth between those two points. Permitted Vendors must be conversant with currencies, with our Promise system, and with Guesting. For this reason, Guesta are not allowed to wear the same hats as residents wear; they go bear-headed or wear individualistic head-coiverings like burkas, mantillas, or mitres. Hats are important here.

Now you see why we adopted donkeys. Kids love to ride in carts, and we move logistics around, back and forth, and the donkeys are busy, and they generate trade.

In winter when the snow is deep, they help move things around when it's difficult for jitneys to get around; so donkeys are our back-up transportation system, and we train them with love and not with cruelty.

Sundries: Harmlessness sells.

Toiletries tend to be herbal, and are usually found at the Laundry where some people make shampoo, herbal and henna conditioners, and skin preparations. (But perfumes have to be brought in, for cash.)

The One and Only Free Lunch

The Big Tent is primarily set up for tourists on weekends in the warm season. It is open starting Thursday from 10am for Coffee, bread and pastries; it begins serving The One and Only Free Lunch at 11:30 until 2:00; Tea, from 2:00 until 4:30.

Co-Op Eatery

Later in the main Dining Tent, Communal Supper (which costs Guests five dollars a person) is served from 5:00 until 7:00. Expect to pitch in and help when you show up if you don't already have a paid Meal pass or can't pay for some reason or other.

The Co-op is not merely the Village Grocery Store, it is where the annual harvest of vegetarian foods is warehoused and preserved, where stable commodities that the Village trades for are trucked in, where community canning and drying occurs.

This is where monks and farmers bring in fresh produce each day, for use and public sale. As the quantities of fresh vegetables growing in our greenhouses is increasing, so also public demand for them is increasing; and there are more people on the Promenade all the time looking for clean organic food.

In the late summer and early autumn, it is a very busy place and probably a third of the Village residents are working in the Co-op or in one of its two large striped tents during that time to put away the harvest for winter.

The Kitchen gets first pick of produce; nobody else can buy until they have picked out what is going to be put up or dehydrated on any given day. Only then--usually by 10am when the coffee shop opens -- can the public come buy theirs. They have to park, as we did, out in the parking lot and take the jitney into the village and then carry out their purchases in shopping bags. That keeps wholesalers out of here.

Big Tent Buffet

The Co-op and its two restaurants share permanent warehouse space (off-site) for stable supplies of commodities--cereal grains, beans, nuts, oil, wine and beer all year long. During our Fall Miracles Show and Festival, meals are served all over the place--wagons and carts and concessions everywhere--and at that time the Co-op dining room is accessible even to our Guests and relatives. But we never reveal or expose where we keep commodities except to say, they're our security against famine.

The Co-op Building is our main "mall" for meals and living essentials during the winter season. It is built for maximum cleanliness and efficient operation according to professional restaurant guidelines.

Tents outside are utilized for sorting and selecting produce during the harvest, but dehydrating fruits and vegetables is done away from hair, birds, bugs and workers with any sign of colds or sickness.

Shopping: Plain clothes

The Co-op building also warehouses household and personal essentials like clothing, linens, blankets, and foul-weather gear. As I said, it's our "mall."

And due to the fact that the Co-op does not charge money to residents for basic, simple clothing, two features become very clear very quickly. The first is that selection is very limited, and that's an understatement.

The Co-op purchases remainders of black and white clothing styles from reputable labels that have not sold for one other reason or another during the regular season so they can be had a rock-bottom prices. All year long we always have gray, black and white sweats duos of soft cotton for anyone who comes here in need of covering. Plain but serviceable. Sweats are available year-round.

Keeping stocks on hand of green cotton, unbleached linens and blankets that we are able to purchase in large quantities is less of a problem than seasonal wear, as are shoes generally; although we have the problem of generally being able to obtain and stock sandals in November and boots in May.

Indeed, everything in the store except underwear is out of season. In the summer the Co-op has winter wear, and in the winter it has summer wear. This is not deliberate or logical, just a fact of the current economy. What this means is that a resident who needs an article of clothing for the current season, a special reason, a color or unusual size must go to a consignment shop and try to get it (used) there or have a tailor make it up specially or find it in a catalog and have it sent out, for cash; but we only have bathing suits in November, and we only have woollies in

May. This is one challenge of village life where poverty rules : so plan ahead.

How do we keep Guests from helping themselves to our free merchandise? The Free Store is only open and available when there are NO Guests on the premises, and Consignment and Crafts merchandise are a way of trading with the local community, our skills and they charge cash. We thought of that. Also, we have three permanent staff making sure State Sales tax gets collected when that applies; who are responsible to and cross-checked at Counting (in the Office).

The fact that Christians have no dress-code means they'll probably tend to buy garments and follow styles that are more colorful and different from residents adhering to Law (black and white); different from Sikhs who live and visit here who wear all-white with turbans; different from monks and nuns who vacation here and wear brown and white or navy and white. And that's just fine. Likewise, tourists have their own dress code; and everybody just points at everybody else and says, 'Look at those funny clothes!'

When we get to the Tailor Shop, I'll show you some examples of garments we produce here simply because they are hard to obtain anywhere else. See, we put on a festivals each year, and costumes are required. So, we agreed that having a Tailor who understands the concept of "wearable art" would work not only for the festivals but also for weddings and formal occasions. So we got that all organized; we loan out costumes and formal wear much as commercial tuxedo rentals do. And the people who create and sew up these festive garments are usually young women from the high school and young mothers who don't want particularly to work in an office or in the kitchens or gardens. They like fashion.

The Hat Dept.

Another challenge of Village Life has to do with the adoption of an appropriate head covering by each permanent resident in the Village. The purpose of the head covering is to show the fact of each individual's participation to all on-lookers. (In the Bible Story, when angels came to Lot without head-coverings, the village men interpreted their appearance to mean they were 'open' to non-traditional or immoral dealings.)

And truly, the fact that incarnate angels tend to eschew head coverings means, no judgments can be made about a person who is bare-headed. It's just that people here are willing to wear head coverings to satisfy an expectation that they are showing up to fulfill certain roles and archetypes except when they are with their intimate Family.

Here, we interpret a visitor's wearing a hat as a visible sign of the intention to fit in and make oneself at home. The absence of a hat has no judgments attached to it. And our having no judgments to go by and no intentions expressed nonverbally means, that person is quite conspicuous here. If that's okay with them, that's okay with us.

The Co-op carries all kinds of head-coverings normally utilized by those who Abide With Favor (live by Holy Law) : yarmulkes, prayer caps, black and white veils and scarves, black broad-brimmed hats, hooded tunics and sweatshirts (for monks), turban-materials (black & white cotton only), baseball caps (black only) white cotton cooks' caps, straw hats. Head-coverings are among those items purchased with Labor Only, along with socks, underwear, leggings and personal care items.

Christians and freemen who follow Angelic Doctrines are free to select working hats from their professions or commercial stores; but all churches and village meetings operate from an expectation that showing up and wearing a hat expressing membership are the same thing.

We're back at Center facing north. Center Field is on your left, so you can never get lost here. This is where we have band concerts, track meets, and Arts and Crafts shows in the warm seasons.

From the Co-op, looking back the way we came--north--across Center Field and across the Street from the Library is a plain-looking clap-board Meeting House and Art Gallery where Sabbath services are conducted for Anabaptist adherents as well as some Buddhists who like the simplicity and lighting of the interior. The Jewish Synagogue has been sharing space with Quakers because their spatial needs are very similar.

The Meeting House/Art Gallery also displays paintings on its walls during the week, and it is transformed by lighting systems for the Sunday Meditation Service, so it is closed as a Gallery on Sundays.

The other six days, sculpture and handicrafts are placed on consignment with an expectation that visitors or tourists will want to buy.

Jake the Tailor is the Quaker whose job it is to manage the displays in between services : put them up and then take those back down that did not sell. He has a shop for mending and alterations and it includes an alternative to dry cleaning that is non-polluting, but you need to ask someone where his door is. It's not very conspicuous, it's not very conspicuous, although if you get to the Pavilion, you've passed it.

Chapel grounds for Liturgical Orders stand at the Exit next to Highway 692 behind the Cloister. This liturgical chapel is modeled after a Trappist Monastery, and it is in use and populated at different times during the week by

Catholics, Anglicans and Orthodox congregants in session..

Finally, the Community Bible Church is situated actually on Highway 692, just outside the entrance on your left. A mainline Protestant church, it serves the larger community also. Nobody's in the business of "being righter" than anybody else. That's silly. We all just realize, we manifest our different gifts in different ways; and we keep our behavior on the "straight and narrow."

Each constituency has its own schedule of activities; however, none of their schedules conflict with the Village rhythm. Rather, they, provide the counter-point to it.

The Rhythms of Community: Y'all come

Life in Diversity has a rhythm as seasons have rhythms, as the sun and moon have rhythms. A schedule of events is at work here which is unstated, as regular as the heartbeat of its children.

There is no list of activities posted anywhere, because everybody already knows that is happening. Just ask. Ask anyone what to see, and you are sure to be invited along and welcomed. You can identify to whom you are speaking by the way people dress; and they will always offer you a place at any activity that is being held in the village, no matter what is going on. Of course, not everyone goes to every activity.

Let me tell you about my life and why I came here. First of all, I always thought it was unfortunate that industry creates "labor saving devices" so people have to go join gyms or buy equipment. That's so lame.

Take our pet situation. Pets need exercise; people need exercise. So, since my "work" is sedentary, I walk two dogs a day, out of the Voc Tech paddocks, that normally guard a field from birds. I just walk over there and they hand me a leash, and I walk two field dogs around the Promenade, twice a day. They get exercise and I get exercise.

Then there's the matter of stairs. Over my head there's a greenhouse that I don't work in because I specialize in computer work. So there is a nice young man who comes here and takes care of all the plants. He has to climb up a ladder to get on the first platform, but there is a cranking dumb- waiter to hoist up materials up there; and there is another ladder going up to the second platform, the one for sprouting seeds. Now, should we have built fancy staircases to get up there? I don't think so. I can make my way up those ladders, and it's some strenuous exercise for me. But then again, I don't have to do it all the time, which Gary does.

Now about dogs again. You know, a significant number of ordinary people are terrified of dogs, and we have a lot of public activities; so here's how we decided to handle our dogs. I have a dog; she is an inside dog, a companion. She can either be in the house with me, or she can be in my very small courtyard, or she can be on-lead walking around the loops with myself or someone else, or she can go to one of four dog-parks, fenced, and play with other dogs--king of the hill, or Frisbee, or get all wet in a pond. Whatever. So, the only dogs that are ever loose are patrol dogs after dark, under the command and control of trained handlers, when the public is not present. We have lots of options to exercise and play with 'em. Make sense?

Monday through Friday the children are in School; and the carpool, dining room and bus service are keeping things moving along from one activity to the next.

The children straggle out of school from 11-3 and go to the Co-op for lunch before they go on to work at apprenticeships the rest of the day, as VocTech students do.

Bus service operates on two five-hour shifts of working residents and guests, usually from 10 am till about 8 pm.. They accept a great deal of help from Students during Summer Festivals and the Annual Gathering.

Co-op

The staff entrance to the Coop is on the back side facing the Car Pool. Each weekday evening at 8pm there is some kind of business meeting.

Mondays, in addition to Labor Unit meetings in individual homes, the Manager meets with Grounds, Needs, and Skills Centers Representatives to deal with guest complaints from the weekend.

Tuesday, the Secretary meets at the Co-op with the Manager, with Counting and outside sources to plan trading for what people need that week.

Wednesday, the Secretary, Clinic personnel, Elder Citizens' Council, and Labor Unit Representatives meet with the Construction Superintendent at his warehouse to deal with housing issues surrounding new residents.

Thursday, there is an Executive Meeting of the Manager, Secretary, Chaplain, and Treasurer at the Library to set an agenda for Sabbath Supper. Things always cycle this way.

The Sabbath

The doctrine of the sabbath is not just a belief, a custom or a tradition. It is the condition of the people to work hard all week and simply kick back on the sabbath day. Since on this planet the sabbath is spread over two days, our custom is to begin Shabbos with the Jewish people Friday night until Saturday sundown; and then finish off so Christians and Sikhs get a Sabbath Saturday night until Sunday sundown. And everyone does this as a cooperative way of resting and trading off responsibilities, together.

The village chaplain/prophet is an "abiding with favor" Judean. He doesn't write, speak or sermonize or prophesy on the sabbath, because what is Law-full is Jews reflecting on God's Sabbath day, when YHVH receives back sufficiency among His people to rest Himself also. So, the prayers of the people at sabbath supper are of Thanksgiving, of acceptance and of reconciliation, of hope, and the offering of one's self as God's friend and companion--NOT begging, pleading or beseeching God to jump through hoops, satisfy preferences, or even listen to the peoples' woes.

On this day, residents adopt being sufficient as the day's doctrine. Woes are saved for Wednesday night singing, healing and prayer services at the Meeting House.

It's time

Shabbos begins Friday at sundown and schoolchildren dress themselves up in costumes of their favored discipline (including ninja, monk, sailor, jockey, or one of the fourteen archetypes of village life), following along behind the uniformed school band, and parade around one of the loops of the Promenade with the town clown and a mime troupe (if one is here that day). They parade for the grounds men, teachers, librarians, the dining room staff, parents and friends (of course). A band concert may pipe in with adult musicians once the parade comes back to center, the athletic field. Everyone is welcome to share Sabbath.

A band itself--and the clowns and mimes--is made up of whoever and musicians who have taken on music as their second vocation out of the love of music and a desire to enrich the life of the village. The only compensation they get is the fun they have and the pleasure they give to audiences, unless their primary archetype is music, in which case they're just doing what they would be doing anyway: making themselves happy.

Children of Christian parents enjoy Sabbath activities as much as anybody, although they observe their Sabbath officially on Sunday (First day) but they're among our most enthusiastic dancers and singers. Since everyone who eats meat eats it on Saturday, quite often Christians will take the initiative to sell hot-dogs and sandwiches on the Promenade on Saturday and relieve Jews Who live by law from the necessity of cooking at all. And then, on Sunday they switch roles; except that now the Christians are eating kosher foods on THEIR sabbath which those abiding by Law have prepared.

Day of Rest

Sikhs are always Vegetarians, and contemplatives (monks and nuns) vary from order to order. Twelve Tribes span our church perspectives. They are Holy Law-abiding Christians, not afraid of liturgy. They teach us how to dance. So, we all have to be open-minded about the matter of food, diet, appearance, doctrines and just do what we can to fit everybody in.

What IS understood is that God gives live animals so that they might live, not die; that wasting animals all the time for food also wastes human life in obesity and disease; that our right time for some of us to eat meat is on the weekend; and that the rest of the week we have taken a vow of poverty, subsist only on what we grow, and avoid judging each other's thoughts and things.

In warm seasons by 5:45 and in cold seasons, by 4:45 the crowd--whoever has shown up for this weekend sabbath celebration--is ready for sabbath supper, so everyone who wants to go to sabbath supper converges on the Co-Op dining room (or tent in the summer) as the jitney arrives with elders and clinic staff.

Next, the musical ensemble begins and plays more restful music during sabbath supper (always a meat meal--the ONLY meat meal on the dining room menu). During and after supper, adults meet and agree on the current events topic for Saturday's library discussion group; and then they move off to the chapel grounds for meditation or a bonfire or candle-lit walk and chanting.

Reflect

Teenagers preside over a bonfire (which symbolizes "letting go" even to small children) and marshmallow roast, either in the Campground (or in the Needs Center, if the weather is bad) until everyone is tired and goes home. (Remember, teenage boys stay out on Sentinel patrols until 2am and then the men take over, so that everyone can sleep in peace.)

Saturday morning hosts a Sikh Sadhana at the Chaplain's geo-home at 4:30 am and meditation hour at amphitheater (60 degrees and above) or the library (59 degrees and below or raining) at 10 in the morning..

The Library, Aviary and Fish Geo-domes are foci of activities all day Saturday. Families are encouraged to visit, watch movies, read the weekend papers, catch up on national news, view their children's displays in the library's gallery, drink coffee or cocoa or tea and relax together.

Relax or Play

Saturday noon box lunches are passed out by a group of volunteer (usually Christians) at midday from the Jitney, which were carefully packed and kept cold by the Co-op (sometimes with the children's help) on Friday afternoon as a clean-foods project for school children. ince hot dogs and barbecue are available in the public square, a box lunch usually contains finger salads or fresh fruit, cheese or nuts and lemonade or V-8 juice, to complement what's sold.

Saturday Afternoon is time for music practice, dancing and testimonies to the victories of our people over grief, lack and sadness. We practice Joy by being active, lively and responsive to music and fun.

At 5-6 pm (depending on the season and the weather) on Saturday all residents, their children and guests gather in the amphitheater for a blessing of the sabbath by the Chaplain; and then, as a company, everyone walks to the dining room, puts on aprons and sets out and serves each other a simple meal of soup, salad and bread. Usually, one loop of houses will coordinate each Saturday supper, and act as hosts and leaders.

Giving Thanks

During the cold season, everyone retires to individual activities, potluck suppers or socializing. Often, churches alternate activities for Saturday night as well. After Saturday supper, those who want to participate or watch improvisational theater head over to the theater; those who want to dance go to the campfire circle or the meeting house; and those who want to chant, go to the chaplain's geo-home.

In the wintertime the women gather for quilting and knitting and the men may gather around the women and just talk. By midnight, everything is quiet again.

Other Holy Days: Personal Holy Days

There are five "personal" holy days here : spiritual initiation, commencement, birthdays, graduation, marriage and the funeral (in which none of us actually personally participates at all) when we're already Gone Home.

The Individual's Village "Role"

It's important that children and adults realize and get comfortable with the roles that are both cut out for them and that they personally choose. A great deal of anxiety is caused by "not knowing what is expected of us." And so it is here, that we put to rest the uncertainty of not knowing. The outcome of this practice is that we lose those--they simply leave--who cannot fit themselves in, who do not want to make commitments, who don't know who they are, or who feel that the necessity to perform one's commitments is beyond their ability."

If you have ever seen the effect of worrying that stalking dogs create in cattle or sheep, you realize behavior becomes markedly defensive under circumstances of great uncertainty. So likewise, families and children worried by abuse or problems are disrupted and there is no way to "act normal."

Hyper-vigilance (and the internal panic and anxiety that create it) is an outcome that both creates disease and leads to failure. This community is about resolving as much threatening uncertainty as possible, and yet still providing options for change and growth.

The first is ***Initiation into one's faith community***. Sometimes this events is called "baptism," sometimes "*bar mitzvah*," sometimes, something else, "baptism of the Holy Ghost," or Confirmation. That's pretty much up to the individual's parents and chosen culture.

The second Holy Day is the ***Commencement Birthday every seven years***. A commencement is an initiation ceremony into each soul's next step of soul evolution. However, intervening birthdays are given simple recognition. A commencement birthday gives a village member the opportunity to make a change in the content and direction of his or her life. While we note that opposites do attract and that marriage mates have every right to change their personal archetype every seven years, we also note with some dismay that many people presume to remain in the same archetype throughout their physical lives. In that case, the commencement ceremony tends to become over-blown birthday party instead of a genuine call to new efforts. Elders see such practice as a waste of time and talent, but there is no way to force change that people don't appear to want.

We don't just choose and adopt our own surnames once in a while; we actually make a commitment to perform in harmony with that archetype, precedent or role that a surname implies. It's not just a name-game of musical chairs. We make a new choice, and that's why it's a "commencement."

Age 7

At age 7 a little girl first articulates the goal of being a wife and mother, so her first Commencement initiates her into the archetype of the Cooks, where she will remain until she is thirteen (but retain the family surname of her mother.)

A 7-year old boy is just becoming aware of his father's archetype, so his first Commencement initiates him into the archetype of his Father, where he will remain until he is thirteen and decide whether or not to retain the family surname of his father.

Age 14

At age 14 a young woman has experienced seven years of taking orders and keeping order; and she now will assert her Preference for an archetype of her own choosing, based on her understanding (and her Teachers' assent) of her Gifts.

If she assumes an archetype other than that of either of her parents, she will take on a new surname, that of her chosen archetype.

At age 14 a young man has experienced 7 years of taking orders and apprenticing to his father, and he now will assert his Preference for an archetype of his own choosing, based on his understanding (and his Teachers' assent) of his Gifts. If he assumes an archetype other than that of either of his parents, he will take on a new surname, that of his chosen archetype.

Age 21

At age 21 a young woman will choose again between the archetype of taking orders and keeping order (as a young wife who takes her husband's name immediately), or she will remain with or adopt a new archetypal vocation based on her understanding (and her work experience) of her Gifts.

A woman may use the surname of her family of birth, of her own archetype, or of her husband.

At age 21 a young man will choose again between the archetype of apprenticing to one vocation, or he will adopt a new line of work based on his understanding and current work experience. It is not uncommon for a man to spend a great deal of time at two or more different kinds of work. There is an archetype for that called a Manager, which will be adopted formally at its appropriate time.

A man may utilize the surname of either of his parents, or of his own chosen archetype. If he chooses to adopt the surname of the archetype of his wife or his wife's family, then he must admit that he is encouraging his wife to enjoy Headship over him.

Age 28

At age 28 a young woman is usually married with one or two children. If she changes her archetype now, it's a sign that the marriage isn't working, and that the Role of her Father now is to find her a new, better-adapted man for herself and her children. At this point, blaming is simply of no use, and the children need to be considered primary, and not everybody's Egos. Better to find out now than later.

If she changes her personal archetype to that of her husband, then her marriage is seen as strong, and her husband is seen as a successful facilitator of his household.

At age 28 (and 35 and 42 and 49) a young man may change his archetype, and change it again and again and again. This may mean he is repudiating the Village system entirely; or it may mean that he is listening to a Spirit, and the Spirit is repudiating the Village. Or, it may mean he is interested in many different activities; and in that case, he may turn out a very competent Manager someday.

The third "Holy Day" is ***Voc Tech Institute Graduation***. That's fairly self-explanatory.

The fourth is a ***wedding*** : a quick hand-fasting, a religious ceremony of promise or an eternal cosmic bond.

Theoretically, a wedding should occur only once. Naturally, there are exceptions.

Any wedding is a ceremony of Promise. That means that the individual bride and groom don't have a CLUE whether things are going to turn out abundantly, sufficiently or not, and usually they trust that God is bringing their marriage to fulfillment--not themselves.

Thus, a decision to marry calls on their ability to make and keep promises, which means, Faith and Faithfulness. Ceremonies are officiated by chaplains, ministers, priests and the fathers of both the bride and the groom, although brothers of the bride have also been known to participate.

A ceremony is organized as a dialogue in which the bride and groom pledge to each other and to the community that they will continue the lifestyle (which is a Holy Promise) of the village; that they will promote the principles of Abiding-in-Favor (if they are Jewish, Anabaptist, Sikh, 7th Day Adventist, Jehovah's Witnesses) or Living-in-Simple Faith (if they are Christians), and that they continually commit themselves to establishing a family focused on the attainment of integrity and harmlessness; they commit to the promise of bearing and rearing healthy children, and of taking care of each other in their old age.

QUERY: What is a HOLY promise? A holy promise is a fundamental CAUSE that drives everything else. It's not an effect. Examples of holy causes : functional DNA, clean water, clean air, clean food are all Holy because these produce healthy people and strong children.

Of and from ourselves, the intention to do good and to tell the Truth, to manifest by sharing and to be happy by caring for others are Holy Causes. These fundamental forces drive society toward good outcomes because individuals at the grassroots level **practice an intention** (without being monitored, told or compelled) to make things work out. That's why these elements ARE HOLY.

Once matrimonial commitments are sealed by ceremony, the couple is free to go off on their Honeymoon, with travel money from the Village Credit Union to help them make their way. The wedding guests then have tea and wedding cake and go home. (No, they don't lay odds or bets. That would be rude.)

The Bride is dressed in a white long dress and silk veil (as a reminder to her new husband that she will forever remain a mystery to him), and the Groom is attired in Black (with white trim) to signify the complementarity of certainty and doubt, strength and weakness, good times and struggle.

The Bride's sisters dress in white also or pale hues and carry the Bride's flowers during the Ceremony. This is to signify the honest intention to support the couple in their married lives. Linen is a good fabric for bridesmaids, and a well-fitted frock can be warn repeatedly, whenever the occasion to state one's good intentions presents itself---even at a funeral.

Black and white are our colors of choice for those of us who came here without money and without price. We work for free to care for others and accept this sign of our financial poverty and interpersonal devotion. But that doesn't prevent us from enjoying richly colored flowers, attractively presented meals or gaily-attired children.

Both the Bride and the Groom keep their growing-up surnames until one of them chooses to adopt the working archetype of the other; and then both of them enjoy the same surname. If the surnames of the two married people remain distinct, then we infer they have a very interesting relationship.

The other Personal Holiday are **Commencement Birthdays** that every resident enjoys every seven years : at ages 7, 14, 21, 28, 35, 42, 49, 56, 63, 70, 77, 84, etc. The purpose of the Commencement at each stage of life is to acknowledge and recognize changes which they, as a Soul, experience through the past seven years of living in community.

The fifth holy day for anyone here is their funeral day. But let's put that off. There is so much to talk about now.

First-Day Activities

Sunday is a busy workday in Diversity. The Sabbath over for residents Abiding by Law (known as Jews), now they turn to business, while Christians observe their Sabbath.

The Chaplain usually likes to co-preach a sermon with or for one of the Christian parishes; or he attends Gudwara with the Sikhs; or he hosts a non-denominational Service at the Geo dome or Chapel grounds at 10 o'clock for visitors, Friends or whomever.

Christians are in church Sunday morning while residents who abide with Law are setting up a flea market at the park to sell extra handiwork for cash to guests and visitors who come practically every Sunday. Tourists come to gape and gawk at residents' odd, plain clothes, much as they gape and gawk at Amish and Sikhs elsewhere. Tourists have cash; and they want to know how such a village is, how Money can be MOOT, and why nobody teaches rules or doctrines here.

The only souvenirs available for tourists to purchase are foodstuffs and "necessaries" in the Co-op (for cash, with work or with equivalent materials), paintings and sculpture in the gallery (for cash or materials), box lunches dispensed by the Jitney (for cash, to replenish the food that tourists and guests consume), and home crafts available in the flea market at the park (for cash only, as an accommodation to Residents who need to generate small cash reserves).

Make a deal

Revenue from all sales accrues to individual accounts; but all monies are processed through OUR credit union so all transactions are transparent. One might ask, how is this village saying they do not deal with money? You see! Here They are taking money, but only as the minority medium.

The natural response to your objection is to say, 'Yes, money is utilized for those expenses for which there is no substitute for money: taxes, telephone service, magazine subscriptions, running shoes. However, Abiding With Favor permits everyone to Survive here without money. Everyone will not have all their Wants met without money; but they will get their Needs met without money. And the Village's modest tourist, and seminar businesses generate the cash necessary to fill in the gap between what is traded for or produced here, and what residents here feel is justified to pay for in cash.

We're developing silk, goose down and wool enterprises, to bolster our economy and serve ourselves at the same time.

Sunday afternoons, it is customary for the Village to hold Competitions on the **The Athletic Field, City Center --** Martial arts, archery, track & field, gymnastics--whatever--mentors and youth have chosen as their gifts. Voc Tech students hold an Engineering Competition, and their machines compete against each other as athletes.

One prize given each year for the best Engineering Design is a scholarship to a good commercial or technical University for the Winner of that competition. Winners of every other kind of competition are offered opportunities to continue or expand their skills, to compete in outside competitions, expenses paid by the Village.

Whereas Guesting is a role of contributing effort in which Promise Notes are never kept, Guests serve as teachers, guides, mentors, actors, musicians; but Artists stick with the promise system due to the real money costs of materials and supplies. Guests are those who arrive with their wit and ability to articulate and trade IDEAS. Each village has its own resident Guests, who come and go a lot due to the fact that they teach regionally or nationally or internationally, or even, inter-dimensionally. Why not?

When an individual qualifies as a Guest, they have mastered trade, barter, promise-keeping, bargaining and simplicity. Their needs are not excessive in terms of preferences although one may require exploratory health interventions for chronic or critical physical problems. These are seniors, after all.

No community can support more than 13% of its population as Guests, including the ones who come to amuse and teach and inspire. But they have physical limitations, so they must be limited as to number at any one time.

During late spring the blue-and-white striped tent serves as foul-weather gym so competitions can occur rain or shine, although the schedule of activities tends to follow weather patterns pretty closely. Thus, track & field events occur in May before it gets too hot; Engineering Competitions are held in early March when it's still very cold and the Tent is just set up.

Groups wanting to display their work sign up months in advance and agree to help with pitching the Big Tent, to have sufficient time to regulate their competitions in terms of Safety, Entertainment Value and Competitive Fairness.

Sunday evening the Village Manager and Chaplain convene a Family Meeting at the Meeting House if any is needed to resolve village disputes or grievances. If no issues arise, they all just walk over to the Chaplain's place for High Tea. As it is written elsewhere:

Your path is like a rock thrown across the expanse.
Not a motion is lost.
There are no spinning wheels, and there is no energy deficit.
All side tracks are part of the Program.

Come on! Here's a Jitney coming by. I wonder why! It's their day off! Let's get on and go around the South Loop.

Beginning the South Loop, in front of you and to your right there is an area of small, raised clapboard houses widely spread apart on this 65-acre section, some having hedges, some with gardens, some with granny-flats attached. These belong--yeah, belong--mainly to Christian families whose men work in Recycling in the Rock Quarry five miles from here, and in the Service Bay at the Car Pool.

These families clearly prefer living spread apart, and they tend to relax on the Sabbath by playing pool and penny-ante poker. Many of them are hunters and fisherman of the archetype Woodsman; and they make a commitment when they move in to hunt and fish with only a camera except on Friday, and to share their bounty with the village on the sabbath. It's also understood that an animal taken for food from up in the woods will also give its skin to our tanner to be tanned and not be squandered.

We do try to find a place for every sort of civil human being, possible.

Get Supper

We have planted chestnut, walnut and maple trees in these sections; some families raise rabbits, chickens and ducks; and wild asparagus, Jerusalem artichokes and blueberries. Perennial crops also keep local families gathering and handling foodstuffs during Fall and Winter months, for Work Credit at the Co-op.

Most other homes--particularly cluster houses--are not surrounded by lawns or gardens because those residents are too busy to deal with yard work and domestic demands.

From here it is hard to distinguish the houses from a hilly landscape or country meadow, and that's how we want it. The condo rules we have adopted do not permit any but unobtrusive exterior colors, do-dads or adornments, for tax assessment reasons, of course. No displays allowed; we all just hunker down.

POPULATION CONTROL--

Village Planning

If Management of a community holds that "We can only afford to support only 13% of our peoples as Elderly and Guest categories, then how do we organize the other 87%? Do we have to do head-counts regularly? No. The other 87% are promise keepers between the age of 14 and retirement age [whenever that occurs]. You know the number of residence SQUARE FEET in the village [because the Village built it all] and their occupancy (210sqft per). You know how many children are showing up at school. You know how many babies were delivered at Heaven's Door, how many pre-schoolers show up at the Laundry DayCare Center occasionally. Everyone is known by name, who resides here, no matter where their physical residence happens to be.

Planning occurs in the Counting Department, and they simply REPORT how many new (21 by 10) living spaces must be built at any time for the number of babies that have been born this year. That's it. Building is "Overhead," to keep safe the creative, imaginative, communicative newborn, young, working, parenting, Guesting population.

So everybody shares information about what, what, when, where, how and why. and confidentiality would kill the whole system; anyone who withholds or skews data IS history.

We expect each marriage-dynasty to produce and/or adopt between 3-to-5 children over a thirty-year period. This represents a doubling of our size, each generation, which is not too large an increase to plan and execute civil growth.

The Woodsmen Group

Men of the Woodsman archetype serve as archers and butchers of the deer herd when it gets too large, and a few of them can kill a steer for the Winter Solstice with a single stroke of a machete-like sword.

The commitment to hunt only during the 26 weeks of autumn and winter is a response to the fact that this our planet has finite resources. If killing occurs everyday of the week, month, year, then there will not be enough animals, enough food to go around. So our residents take a Vow of Poverty, to limit their killing to six months of hunting Fridays per year except during a real food scarcity. And they take turns providing only sufficient meat for Sabbath suppers--that is presently about 50 pounds of meat per week not counting domestic animals we raise.

Killing is not an activity that gets a lot of public attention in the Village. Most residents are embarrassed by the fact that killing occurs at all, here. Yet the Law permits people to eat meat on the Sabbath; so somebody has to do it, whether the animals are rabbit, fish, lamb, steer, or fowl. Young calves are mercifully never killed as 'veal.' Pigs in the Village only serve as Sentinels, not as 'pork,' because pigs are very intelligent animals like dogs are; and intelligent mammals should not experience being sacrificed for food. That's how we define food versus non-food animals :

if they're aware enough to be trained to do something useful to us, they are not available as a food animal except in a dire, life-threatening emergency such as a general famine during winter when nothing can grow.

There are paddocks behind VocTech where sacrificing animals occurs; and a prayer of surrender and thanksgiving is offered over each animal(s) before it is killed for its meat, bones and skin. Every effort is made to inflict as little discomfort on the animal as possible. Only youngsters over the age of fourteen are permitted to witness butchering animals, because smaller children identify with the animals and become frightened of Death.

External & Devoted Gardens

Now on your left is a gradual sloping hill that hides one Cluster; but behind that (and what you can't see yet) is a trombe wall for a large set of greenhouses along the path facing southeast, with cultivated fields on the opposite side. In the wintertime, residents use this first greenhouse for team sports like volleyball and basketball; competitions in marshal arts, gymnastics, dancing.

Between the Winter Solstice and the Spring Equinox, lights are on in the Greenhouses to extend daylight hours and permit growing fresh tubers practically all year; thus, it makes sense to utilize extra light generated to promote year-round sports and exercise among active people who like both to help in the garden and keep physically fit. (One of the exercise machines we have is a bicycle-generator, in the middle greenhouse, to help with generating power for lighting and telephone service here.)

Most residents eat about a pound of greens and half a pound of tuber per day in spring, each. It's the job of the Greenhouse to provide the tubers. Also, the Greenhouse keeps supplies of fresh herbs and garnishes to liven up the

Dining Room's rather drab winter menu. Perennials normally vulnerable to cold weather are also kept here: fragrant roses, star jasmine, globe artichokes, pea vines, 6 lemon trees and 6 orange trees, and we're trying this year to establish our first banana tree in this particular greenhouse next to the trombe wall. We'll see.

Greenhouses have the same staffing year-round, because plants they contain are perennials, and the staff are most familiar with caring for them. But during summers, a few spouses of field hands will also work here; and during winters when it's too cold to grow anything outside, a few die-hards volunteer to work getting new plants ready for spring planting.

Mostly, though, we have to snare people who come to exercise as helpers when there is really heavy work to be done. There will be a fish-farming Biosphere located here also when we build one, due to the inevitability of an unpleasant Odor. [Local residents insisted that fish farming be located out away from everything else.]

Encouraging Residents to work in fields is not a great problem, because no one ever needs to work physically more than three hours at a stretch (instead of the customary, four for other functions) between April and October. Rubber slickers and boots are available for bad weather, box lunches are provided by the Dining Room Jitney, and work is organized as a neighborhood outing rather than as a strict duty-roster.

The more mature members of the village come trekking out here each day, to select their favorite items for the cook to prepare, and to preclude the necessity of anyone else's having to serve as their harvester on that day. It is considered a matter of pride, to bring one's own food--gathered, grown and sacrificed--to the village Table.

Most ground cultivating is done by pigs and utilizing portable fencing to keep them confined where uprooting and trampling is good for working new mulch into the soil.

Six Residents each day (those who are known to be able and willing) from each of the six neighborhoods alternate field work, one day's work each third day, except the Sabbath, when nobody works. Usually, there's a picnic after each 3-hour shift, and anybody who wants to work both shifts in a day (a total of 6 hours) doesn't have to come back for a whole week. Most people simply schedule the same 2-shift day every week for the 26-week season, so they can have lunch or dinner with their friends from another neighborhood and get their work commitment out of the way at the same time.

(What this means is that each able-bodied adult expects to work in the fields a maximum of 26-6-hour days per year to gather all the fresh food the Village needs for the summer and fall, for an equivalent of $1560 in 2005 wages.)

Cooperative HarvestFarm fields we harvest are organized as raised beds 18" high with crushed rock paths between because most of the Residents are amateur gardeners who dislike getting muddy or bending over too much. The 18" height makes it simple and easy to cultivate, weed and harvest the kind of flowers and vegetables that the Village tends to prefer: corn, tomatoes, peppers, peas, onions; sunflowers, marigolds, petunias, nasturtiums, alyssum (for bees), and lilies and fragrant flowers for churches--stock, lilacs, and mock orange.

A few specimens of fragrant roses we keep here are available also, with all the greens that must be grown year-round. Greens are always and only grown in greenhouses so supply is stabilized and wandering animals never are a factor in our food distribution.

The monks and nuns at our Cloister have their own greenhouses as part of the way they support themselves. Like everyone else, each contemplative does three hours community work to support their Order in the village.

A good supply of water for the garden is available at the Main Water Head [fountain] from the creek, that is tapped off also by our swimming Pond. We adopted rain-barrel and cistern conservation of rainwater, but it is not sufficient. Further, we're concerned here, that groundwater has been testing heavy with contaminants. We chose using hand pumps and gas-pumps with hose connections rather than running water pipes all over our town. What this means is, we're dependent on rainfall or cistern storage for water to irrigate the entire field of raised beds quickly and easily in dry seasons.

Appearance of the garden is neither a matter of Vanity nor embarrassment; it is a matter of utility. In between each set of raised-beds you will see large dug-outs filled with piles of decomposing plant materials and manure, and piles of new aerated soil, all covered with open plastic netting, to eliminate blowing around and any growth of molds caused by lack of oxygen (acid condition of the soil).

After each annual harvest a winter cover crop is planted; after that crop is gathered and the plants have been mulched over, pigs are fenced into the area to cultivate it for the next growing season in the spring. Pigs are great for cleaning out a planting bed of weeds, trampling it over and fertilizing it. This way, no human has to work a plow in the Village, and our soils get all the fertilization and cultivation they need. Besides, the pigs have a good time.

Consistent evaluation of the soil suffices if the raised-beds are clean of weeds, moist and not breeding insects or molds. Mulch provided by Grounds men (who mow and prune Center Field, the Formal Park and around the Library) by a weekly garbage-recycling detail deposit mulch in piles alternating with the raised rows of plants.

Once it has all fermented together sufficiently to kill all seeds and pathogens, it is mixed and aerated with vermiculite for the next planting cycle. (The reason mulch is located right next to the planting beds is to minimize the smell for nearby residents and to maximize ease-of-use when it is ready.)

Birds always challenge the farm by robbing seeds and grains from fields during the sowing season. Our solution is to direct several Sentinel dogs to patrol fenced fields surrounding their doghouses (which are portable) until the seeds can sprout. The dogs have a good time routing birds until plants have become hardy. The presence of their doghouse for some reason alerts the dog to the need to evacuate **elsewhere** so we have few problems with dog droppings on our new plants so long as the dogs get to patrol regularly--elsewhere--and leave their treasures far from their 'territories.' Dogs thrive with prompting and supervision anyway, so their regular "coffee-break rotations" are no problem, to keep the fields clean.

Field-sitting

As I said before, the Faith Church, built of concrete blocks, clapboards and whitewashed by the members themselves is over there by Highway 692. You can see the back of it. One wonders why the Faith Church didn't put up more of a fuss about smells of these organic fields from here. Yet perhaps their claim to be Fishers of Men is more Fact than Fiction because this Church has staunchly supported both the way we mulch plants and the idea of fish-farming from its inception. Their members are the ones who keep bringing in fish they catch to Sabbath. I guess they just like fishing; or they don't like fishing. I'm not sure.

Now the Jitney circles around, and you can see fields for truck gardening. The yield of these fifty-six acres varies as the gardeners in charge experiment with different varieties of seeds and different rotations of crops. Usually a winter-wheat crop or a cover crop of legumes are turned under by Sentinel pigs in early spring.

Large-scale trucking-in of foods and perishables isn't practical for a Village Economy, because spoilage demands refrigeration and packaging, both great polluters of the environment. So we here grow what we want to eat everyday: greens, tubers, and pungent vegetables. Nuts, fruits and berries are harvested in other neighborhoods. Dairy products are available daily from our own Dairy in spring in summer. Cheese, eggs and nuts fortify the children for winter months and hard work.

Abiding With Favor people eat meat occasionally on the Sabbath, principally culling small herds of herbivores which live on the property: 8 steers, 6 goats, fish from the creek. Wild rabbits, squirrels and deer that wander onto Village lands looking for food in the wintertime are safe from harm if we can feed them, or dinner, if we cannot feed them.

Products grown, processed or made in the Village are baskets, candles, dried herbs, feather art (out of the aviary), ginseng roots, graphic arts, jams & jellies, needlework, nuts & nut butters, potpourris, pottery, knitted and crocheted garments and afghans. These are on display for sale at the Meeting House and in the Co-Op. "Down" and silk production are being added to this list, as we breed strong geese and propagate silk worms.

Leather from four steers a year that we sacrifice is not sufficient to make shoes for everybody. We have adopted the policy of trading for or buying shoes, and we use what tanned leather we get to make our own leather harnesses and satchels because they are expensive to buy, in cash.

It has taken only a short time to drive the circuit today, because the jitney has not made its usual stops to pick up or drop off school children and pets, deliver milk, mail and packages, pick up trash and exchange articles for the residents who share with and borrow from each other. Even the Library uses the Jitney to deliver books which Residents call up and request. Now we are back at where we started; this loop returns us to the Library and Chaplin Theater, but then proceeds past another row of cluster-homes into the main service area to the west, where we keep building materials. That area isn't really developed yet.

On the other side of the materials yard is a Dairy farm of about 60 acres. It's run independently by a Dan Martin and his family, Mennonites, and they trade and barter with the village residents freely. The deal we cut with him is this: he gets 60 acres and sufficient forage and water for his herd of 40 cows, and we get 25% of his milk production which we pick up [about 16-20 gallons a day] in sterile 5-gallon containers. What Dan can't sell on the open market he trades back to us as Cheese in return for other services we provide to him.

We also have a two-story Bunk House opposite the Carpool for temporary workers and tourists who don't want to camp. It's white and it's down past the Car Pool, one of the few buildings that were already here when we took over this property.

One thing, Friend : You don't want to run out of gas in this place; they charge a days' work for just one tank of 94-octane gas (94-octane is the only kind they sell). And the reason they do so is to discourage motoring entirely on the property. A gas-run car only holds about eighteen gallons of fuel, so that is a stiff penalty for gas-engine cars. An electric hook-up costs the same, but the 'range' of an electric car is much greater than one of the local gas engine models. We're eagerly awaiting some new technologies to diminish our need for gasoline.

Most maintenance men and service workers live in Family homes immediately south of the service area where we drove by in the Jitney, so they walk to work like everybody else. Occasionally, you will see one of them who lives out past the Greenhouse riding on the jitney, but I think they are embarrassed to be seen on it, as if it is not 'manly' enough to accept a lift.

It's a good thing that the mortician, Lenny, is an easy-going guy, because his Mortuary is located directly across from the pool hall. When things are quiet for him, Lenny typically hangs around and plays a mean game of pocket-pool and he notices whether somebody has a problem getting home after a few games of pool and a few beers. He tries very hard to work himself out of business.

Menfolk on this side of the village tend to separate themselves by archetype into touch-football and baseball teams, horseshoe tournaments and hunting twosomes. They call themselves Woodsmen, Wolf Pack or Tigers. It doesn't matter whether the men themselves are scholars, managers or maintenance men. What one notices is that most of their competitiveness is within their groups, not between groups. This is because they acknowledge and recognize the Separateness of village archetypes, as we all must.

Men at Play

The purpose which men's groups serves is to relieve and energize their Egos; and it is most desirable to accomplish energizing the men without the effects of excessive alcohol, so men can take their 'high spirits' home to their wives. Any healthy woman loves to be charged up by her rowdy husband.

Some Christians permit drinking alcohol outside of the Communion table, and therefore, beer and wine cannot be forbidden to grown men in the Village. They are available at the pool hall and the Black Boar Cafe, a bottle of beer or a glass of wine with a sandwich or a meal.

You see, our Center Field where we hold athletic events as well as regular Flea and Crafts Market sales has a wide-open feel. Cultivated fields are to the south of us, the Cloister off to the Right is set on a hill, and Sharing School is in front of us. This large grassy field is the very Hub of community life in summertime.

Behind us to your right, at the very southernmost border of our property, we grow kudzu as forage for animals and berries as a boundary. And due to the fact that there are always animals relatively loose on the property, pedestrians in that area are provided secured pathways for protection from surprises or intrusions by roaming quadrupeds. You can see animals at distance from here sometimes but we've been screened off, hedged, bridged over, or detoured around them. but heaven help you if you get in their way, and you sure wouldn't want to have to cut your way through the kudzu patch. So, we plant kudzu where there are raised wooden pathways built over grazing areas to protect people from animals, muddy feet, twisted ankles (if someone were to step in a hole) and snake bites. Of course we have snakes here. They eat rats that hide in kudzu. We actually encourage and breed black snakes to dominate the area. Harmless to us and our children--very timid around humans--they prey on other snakes and rats and they are easy to spot and conserve.

Indeed, we do not want our children ever to be timid nor afraid of animals. God did not create animals to torment us; rather, to be stewarded and utilized to their fullest potentials. So the only animals you will deal with here are those that have been socialized to be harmless in human groups, among babies and frail elderly in public places.

Sharing School

Learning Is Functional

The work-job of children here in Diversity is civilizing, socializing and learning how to discern correct information from fantasy; learning to express themselves and to save their best thoughts for the future.

Sharing School lies half-way up the East hill next to the Town Park and Elder Apartments. The school looks like a wheel, with five 'spokes' consisting of classrooms attached to a geodesic-dome where a large media center and testing area is always quiet.

From the main Promenade walking by our Cloister, all you'll see is its tile roof where it nearly meets the sod on the street side so it looks like a lumpy field of wildflowers with a roof on it when we're walking by. A paved playground and parking area are back behind, up a long driveway; on that side it looks more conventional.

On top of the school berm there is a playground for small children; but the larger and older students use their parking lot or the central Athletic Field for their physical activities.

All students share in the care of the school building as well as grounds and gardens. Each class designs and cares for the garden adjacent to its Home Room. Naturally, younger children opt for a simple design, but they get a great deal of pleasure out of seeing last-term's design in full-bloom when they return to School in the Fall.

Growing Up Together

School is held from the middle of Harvest (September 1st) until after planting has been completed in late spring (May 15th) for four hours a day, five days a week (Monday through Friday).

In summer, when everyone is busy weeding and training plants, or with sports, vacations and festivals, the only continuing requirements for the children to keep are to write in a Working Journal every day, to make bag lunches for their families, and to adapt themselves to Spirit by working in Silence for two hours per day at whatever they are given to do.

Sharing School presently has seventy-three children attending full-time, of whom twelve are Christians; and it is also serving forty-three adult learners continuously on a quarterly basis year-round. The adults take classes for eleven each quarter if there is a project and a discipline which they are trying to master.

Each class of the six classes of children holds two grades, odd and even. Grades 1&3 are together; 2&4 are together; 5&7, 6&8; 9&11; and 10&12. This break-out provides a truly symbiotic relationship between students. Unless they're having some kind of problem, they can adopt and keep the same learning-teams throughout their school careers.

Teachers explain to the older ones, and illustrate how spirituality underlies all reality, how it is the electronic template by which life propagates. Older students explain things to the younger ones; and younger ones help the older ones with the more boring, mundane tasks required in each project. In this way, students learn to follow and to lead, every day.

In truth there is not, in all the philosophies in all the world, a way to restrain the private life and habits from secret vice, without a solid belief in and realization of the Eye of God seeing all things and thoughts.

"Liking"

Children's progress operate best from the understanding that children do best what they feel like doing; they enjoy selecting things that interest them; they like to memorize rules and recite them before others;like to figure things out; and so this is what the School begins with, what they like. And their teachers seek to discover each child's form of Guidance, and encourage what is Good that they inwardly initiate.

Having opportunities to initiate the thoughts that come to them, they have no use for deception and deceit. Everyone seeks their own internal and highest light, and works from that light, to create what is good.

Deceit is not merely discouraged; it is sternly punished; lies and obfuscations are exposed and revealed; tricks are overturned; ridicule is contradicted; teasing is forbidden; conspiracies are sufficient reason for expulsion.

Children who are NOT actively ascending are descending; standing still is the same as sliding backward. So, teachers are moved to prod, challenge, provoke and listen very deeply to their charges, to discover their gifts.

It is thought each soul must turn his attention inward, to himself or herself, becoming a constant magistrate, sitting in judgment upon himself or herself (and in the all-seeing eyes of God, our Father who seeks our success) as to thoughts, works and behavior. This is why journaling is the primary tool of literacy in the Village; THE inner tool of self-reflective Justice.

We also teach building and gardening. The ancients built their temples so durable that succeeding generations forgot the art of building. Better it is for talent to remain, than for stones and pillars of iron to remain.

Instead of one teacher instructing all students, our students journal what they discover out of their own experiences and research; and they share what they journal with their contemporaries. In this way they all learn to lead and all learn to follow each other's leadings. And the teacher serves as facilitator and Leader to new knowledge by questioning facts, questioning data, questioning intention, questioning motive. (Needless to say, Teachers have a childlike disposition and curiosity is their primary Gift.)

The school Day promotes ***five*** broad primary skills:

FOCUS: To observe number, size, shape and characteristics of real and abstract things and thoughts;

To focus hearing so that one can articulate activities in the Village without having to see them;

To focus vision so that one can find all his needs in the visual diversity that exists in the Village without having to ask things to be pointed out.

INITIATE: To locate the boundaries of their present knowledge and know when to SEEK more information and where to find the information they need;

PONDER: To think critically about the information they are sifting through, for sequential order, salience, coherence, consistency and harmony with visible effects and outcomes.

RECORD: To write down what is salient to their Problem or issue, so the data and explanatory information itself becomes the tool and a task sequence needed to satisfy its solution (understanding) as well as provide a desirable outcome from the learning.

IMPLEMENT: To take one's information, the options presented, the obstacles to overcome, and to build a reality out of this knowing, whether it's a bird cage, a report, a meal, a garment, a remembrance, a token, a gift or a sacrifice of oneself, consciously assented to.

* * * * *

The school day is organized to naturally progress the children through these experiences without time limits or bells. Complicated theories are eliminated, and words are simply taken at face value. The children are doing what they need to learn how to do, and activities are naturally flowing from one function to the next as needs of the children arise and diminish.

The fact that children come to school from different ways of thinking provides a great enrichment to their education. The fact that some children wear only black and white, some wear turbans, and some wear standard colored clothes and jeans means that the differences which the children carry around in their heads is reflected on the outside. Thus, the whole system is honestly working to portray diversity, it doesn't just give lip- service to Diversity.

In terms of race, the children who AbideWithFavor derive from mixed races, Christians tend to be of mixed races, and Sikhs tend to be Caucasian and Indian.

In terms of families, many Village children are orphans and foster children whose parents have dropped them off here, due to hardship or illness. In terms of age distribution, most of our adult residents are past 40 and have grown children who live elsewhere. The reason we have so many children is that our mature residents have taken on the responsibility to raise abandoned children who appear to have promise of integrity.

God gives us our children just as He gives us our crops, in due season. The only stipulation that prevents a child from being accepted and adopted by one of our resident families is the presence of some communicable diseases in their blood test, which our clinic will administer several times, just to be sure. There are some diseases we simply cannot accept into our midst.

Children come to school by age group, 8am for first and third grade, 8:30 for second and fourth, 9 o'clock for fifth and seventh, 9:30 for sixth and eighth, and so on, so that the last of the high schoolers wander in about 10:30.

This starting up schedule conforms to children's natural tendencies, so there is no resistance to coming to school. The schedule also implies that we expect our children to be able to walk to school on their own, unassisted, and that the experience of walking to school, itself, is valuable. Therefore, we made certain that is a safe experience, safe from every sort and form of predation and/or danger, safe as we can make it.

Straggling in is very important. The process gives each homeroom teacher an opportunity to meet one-on-one with each student as s/he arrives, to spend about ten or fifteen minutes checking over the previous day's math operations, the day's Working Journal entries, penmanship for Life Journal entries, check on selections for the next public reading or play, the last test point, the next test point, and the next outside project (which will be displayed at our Library or Meeting House for everyone to see).

All of each student's work is seen as very important to the child and to the community. Inspirations which children receive are seen as just as important as those which elders receive in prayer and meditation. All schoolwork is seen as sacred and appropriate preparation for a vocation to come. And ten years after we have done our work with our children, we find out just what they are made of.

During Check-In, the student's attitude is also observed and inferred from his or her appearance, vitality and ability to center and to focus. There is no such thing as a bad attitude, although there are problems with fatigue caused by anger, ego, denial, guilt, and fears around expectations and behavior.

When a child begins to doubt Village ways, to press for Change, e.g., to cut their hair short, demand different attire and the freedom to go other places, then the teacher gently notices the parents and the elders that this child will need space for a time until any decision about vocation or mission can occur.

Rebellious adolescents are the rule here rather than the exception. Giving space to their need to individuate is the primary responsibility of the parents and family.

If a child chooses to resign from AbidingWithFavor, then s/he also needs to know what other options exist and how they can be identified and what good can be expected from LivingWithSimpleFaith or Living Autonomously. If and when a child chooses lawlessness (by will-full behavior), s/he may even find the way back someday with God's Help.

Sometimes, God permits disruptive people to help bring about Change. Justice works to confirm or release one's commitment to AbideWithFavor in the Village--nothing more and nothing less.

Attitude

Sometimes for a listless child, hot cocoa helps; sometimes they need to walk or jog a lap around the promenade; sometimes all it takes to get them focused is offer them a foot massage, and they will quickly transform themselves rather than suffer such an indignity.

If nothing works to revive their sunny disposition, the child is taken to the clinic, on foot or by jitney, for a check-up and a short rest while mom is called. After check-in each child goes to the morning room for Breakfast.

Breakfast accounts for a significant part of each child's education. It involves simple hand skills, leadership skills, a sequence of steps to arrange the dining room, the process of choosing and preparing the breakfast itself, including reading and following directions, weighing, measuring, assembling, using electricity and gas stoves; and keeping everything clean.

Due to most residents taking lunch and dinner at the Cafe and Dining Room, there are only rudimentary kitchens in the homes of those who AbideWithFavor. Cooking is a shared community activity-- not a solitary task. (Christians tend to have more elaborate kitchens.) Most parents put together a simple breakfast out of their pantry, and the children are fed at school in the morning. So the teaching of Breakfast One-A is the children's initiation into community's life. Making breakfast becomes the metaphor for cooperating in the community at all levels.

By 8:45 the children have sat down to breakfast, so that by 9:00 the first public reading can begin. Public readings (reading aloud to the assembled group) are honored milestones won by students who are constantly searching for what is interesting.

Children will tip-toe in and sit down quietly, because one of their classmates today will read his/her Work and commentary, and move on to their next Station. They will eat quietly and clear their dishes quietly because they don't want to miss how Janie or John got by Mrs. Purcie's criticism this time.

Early in the day, public readings will give a new reader a chance to recite a simple poem or read a well-practiced story; but later on, as the older students arrive in the breakfast room, the readings will begin to take on more critical thinking skills and rhetorical leanings. After hearing the Public Reading for one's own Class, it's time to go to the Math Lab.

Formal Classes

Math Lab operates for all 73 students from 9am to 1pm, and students straggle in from breakfast. Early in the day, the Math Lab is working finger puzzles, following logical operations, drawing geometric shapes, and reciting arithmetic drills. Later on, when the teenagers arrive, they will work in CAD programs to compute and graph volumes, velocities, trajectories, and percentage compositions tables. Those at the Skills Center will work on calculating the value of work, costs of materials and determining the margins needed to keep the Village safe. Elders at the end of the day will deal with number theory and functions.

At the end of each math task and practice, there is a contest to test command, speed and accuracy of verbal computations. The winner of each competition gets to choose a challenge, a special teacher, a special project, even a class field trip. Some children win at Math; some win at Spelling; some win at Debate; some win at Track & Field; some win at Mechanics. Winning always gains opportunities; it does not gain mere prizes, baubles or things to tack on the wall.

From the Math Lab, students wander over to the Media Center (just before or just after Lunch) to work on their own next public reading or debate in groups and individually. When they arrive, they may take a turn listening to others reading and to a teacher's kind and helpful comments; and then they pick up a book and read to the class for about 10 minutes themselves, until enough of the book has been read aloud that a discussion of the material would be a profitable exercise. Teachers facilitate discussions so everyone gets an opportunity to chime in.

Teachers acting as facilitators chair round-table discussions of the elements and issues in the story that was read. Each participant in the discussion records new vocabulary words in his/her cumulative glossary and makes appropriate notes for the application of these concepts to their journal-writing class which follows.

(Teachers hold an expectation that each child will carry the understanding from one class to an application of that concept in the next class, to reinforce learning; and teachers compare notes to make sure that happens.

Research and journal writing are the primary modes of cooperative learning in this school system.)

As a school, a group of teachers and as parents, we want our children to thoroughly understand some of the paradoxes they will face in real life. After the age of approximately eleven, children are introduced to the field of sorting out conflicts and disputes. One way we do this is through discussion and application of paradox theory :

* "Do to and for others what you want them to do to and for you." *Ergo*, A life devoted to our own happiness yields misery; and a life devoted to the care and happiness of others yields happiness.

* "Familiarity breeds cohesion not Truth necessarily."

* "A rose by any other name is still a rose; and a thorn by any other name is still a thorn." Also, "Sticks and stones may break my bones; but names will never hurt me," is the corollary.

* The reality of family life is, the people we love drive

us crazy if we don't agree on limits and boundaries (rules) set on behavior.

* "All generalizations are at least partially false, including this one."

After discussions students straggle out of the Media center because they are tired of sitting and want to play some games: hop scotch, four square, obstacle course, kick-ball, basketball.

If it's raining outside, books and spatial games are available, equivalent to Chess, Solitaire, puzzles, checkers; or an impromptu band concert or rounds singing can be organized, for a brief recess.

Demonstrations

After Recess in the Media Center, students are compiling facts and interpretations for entry into their Life Journals, or they are practicing careful penmanship. Penmanship is given great Value, because it expresses an individual's value for clarity and the desire to be Understood.

Being able to articulate and record one's thoughts is an operation of great trust in God's Spirit and trust in the community to safe keep private records and journals. Each person records his and her own set of textbooks, to hand down from one generation-to-the-next-generation. Every resident maintains a yearly life journal, to save the best of themselves for their progeny.

While it is true that we receive from the Subjective Dimension [Heaven and Hell] our best and worst thoughts, it is what we put into practice and make public about our Soul Progress that makes us what we are.

It is what we consent to DO [not merely think] is what accrues judgments about our character.

Thus a Journal is a testimony to our intentions, our ideals, and our way of being in this physical life. To neglect saving our best thoughts is also to neglect socializing our children, edifying ourselves in bad times, and reviewing prior experiences when memory dims. We do this because each and every person in this community is a Child of God. God speaks to His children, so every resident in Diversity keeps a careful record of his/her thought experiences, revelations, interpretations, and on-going dialogue with God the Father. Quite often, "behavior" is the topic of dialogue in one's journal.

Our Journals are precious, and they are referenced and kept (once a blank book is filled) throughout a person's life in the Library. They can be referred to in times of stress or disputes, or in the case of sudden absence or Death, by family members. However, they are considered confidential, so they can only be read with written permission of

the author; or in case the author is deceased, with permission of his or her family.

Experience & Wisdom
Identifying and Correcting Behavior :

"Ye shall know the tree by its fruit."

Abuse accompanies continual stress. When we were in the world, most of us experienced abuse; otherwise we would not have sought safety and come to live where safety is greatly valued. But scars remain; and hidden vices remain. And fears remain.

Sometimes we don't even want to remember how bad it was; and that makes healing very hard to accomplish, and forgiveness very far away. There are indicators when a person is being abused that are visible by all. Jealousy and unrealistic expectations are abusive.

Anxiety is the indicator.

Isolation is an indicator of shame. Bickering is an indicator of the inability to negotiate limits and boundaries. Any use of force to instill control is an indicator that the spirit is broken, uproar is at work, and no reasonable argument will be heard.

So, we watch for these indicators. And persons who demonstrate indicators are placed "on reproof" and they are shunned until they leave. We simply do not permit anger to take hold of our children for the sin of mistreatment. They will have plenty of other reasons to be angry in the world where cruelty, waste and carelessness abound.

A person who gets stoned or drunk is simply led away to a hut or tent in a field until he or she gets re-sensitized to limits and boundaries. If living there is less stressful than living in community, then they can stay out in the elements, gather their own food, work for their needs. But there is no purpose in creating a community and having some people space out because they can't stand community obligations, roles and manners.

If one needs to space out in order to "stand it" here, then that one needs to be someplace else.

From a legal standpoint, the Village operates from the principle that all thoughts are legal (perhaps not disciplined or wise or logical) until they produce effects which disturb or disrupt another person such that someone complains to Elders about their indicators of silent vices.

In that vein, however, we do require every resident to keep a journal and log their work products accurately. If anything is found missing, journal entries are requested as testimony. IF it is discovered that an individual's journal reflects fantasizing or getting even or disrupting things, what that says to the Elders is--at the very least--subjectively and psychically, that person is in need of healing.

We all self-examine to see why and how some deficiencies are cropping up. And when some resist healing or refuse to be accountable, then perhaps their Right Place is not in This Place. And so, this is how the community keeps safe : we expel anyone who manifests indicators of abuse, violence, greed or covetousness on the second incident. Their personal belongings are packed up for them and they are delivered to the nearest Greyhound bus depot with $50 to go wherever they want to go--out.

From the standpoint of keeping an orderly and peaceful village, the use of a journal as evidence of intention is crucial because journals always divulge the secret person of the heart. A person who has become disturbed will be exposed when their journal is read. And that's that. That's the "why" of journaling and of carefully librarying journals.

It's impossible to write a whole-souled testimony-in-journal and do harm to anyone without any contradictory indicators showing up.

After some progress has been attained in the Daily Journal, each student returns to homeroom to retire their work and request admission to their favorite project, exercise, craft or discipline.

Some students request music, some carpentry, some want baby-care; but all the students will go to an assigned volunteer teacher (who also needs to work for village credit) after they have lunch at the Co-op, and they will complete a project or series of projects with that single teacher.

Students may select two projects per calendar quarter (Fall quarter or Winter quarter) to master; and most of them select projects which give both learning experience AND some village work credit for their fulfillment.

Investing SEED Efforts

Behind Voch Tech Institute we support the development of three internal industries. To assure a secure supply of warm clothing for ourselves, we are breeding Canada geese for meat, sentinel duty and down production; and we are learning to cultivate the silk worms and produce our own silk.

We also have a group of women working with shepherds to prepare wool for dying and weaving cloth. Yet these new enterprises demand some years of propagating and supporting flocks, silk moths and geese before we can even begin substantial production.

In the meantime, this village trades produce and flowers to the local communities for other articles -- stockings, fabrics from fibers we cannot yet produce ourselves; coffee, herbs and teas unnatural to this locale. But we grow our own tobacco for the men's sweat lodge. Men smoke and drum; but women tend to lounge in the spa, get their hair colored and done, have their nails buffed shiny and relax by creating their own simple clothes with needlework. Elders often participate in these ventures.

We have come nearly all the way back to the Entrance--that way--and straight ahead of us is the Loop where the Formal Garden and Memorial Wall are located.

To our left, now, we're back at the Library and Amphitheater. So you're looking at the back of the Library from here and the Amphitheater is behind us where you can see a group of children climbing around the separated terraces.

Film Library

Because films have sound and the sound room is not complete, we are using a temporary mobile Film Library here, for films, videos and music. Here we archive and keep track of records, tapes, videos and personal Journals, all of which are considered to be "personal property of the owner." The process of checking something out is not unlike a bank safety deposit box.

Chaplin Theater is behind the Library, where films are shown on Saturday evenings for groups, and during the week, for individuals. This is because showing to groups requires a lot more clean-up and supervision, that we just don't have available during the week.

Another rotunda--a glass biosphere--will supplement the Library's current crowded quarters, we hope soon. It will not affect operation of the Theater and Library, but it will have to be located up by Elders' apartments because there's no room at the monastery, which sits on the highest point in the Village.

There are hopes to adapt the new Library for a planetarium also; but means and materials for that project haven't shown up yet.

There is always dissension about planting more--or fewer--trees along Promenade around the Library because more trees provide more shade; but they also create mess that grounds men have to clean up. The major complaint is that there are never enough grounds men to keep the village mowed, clipped, and cleaned out in its most public places.

The supervisor is a gentle philosopher by nature, and a good example to the other men, but he does not wield a strong discipline, so the people at meeting tend to favor low-maintenance plants and trees that don't drop leaves, sap, bugs and pods on people and on the street and on the cars--even if evergreens are not as pretty as deciduous varieties.

The Amphitheater was built by the Aeonion monk cloister, as part of their Temple worship, in a classic Greek, outdoor style except it's glassed over so we can utilize it in very cold weather comfortably.

Utilized for worship and funeral services for the whole community, it is built of quarried stone because monks knew how to get and quarry stone. The monks let kids plant new annuals each year, on its periphery.

Nearly at the end of our walk, across the street to your right past the Formal Park and church in front of you with Sharing School behind us, there are apartments for independent Elders and Aged Residents.

Elders live in tri-clusters closest to the Clinic and the 'outside world.' Their backyard, unlike other homes with decks or spread-out yards faces the Formal Garden that also backs up to Central Park Playground. The Village swimming pond and sand field (for volleyball) are right here that elders oversee also.

While they like to work in and around the Formal Garden to keep it spotless, they can also attend to and supervise swimmers in the civic pond. It works to have Elders responsible for safety here, because they tolerate little mischief, noise or horseplay.

The pond is kept clean for swimming by constant filtering even though it lies at the bottom of the hollow and receives water from several creeks. Water having passed over stone creek beds is clean and pure and needs no chlorination. There is an overflow valve for the pond that diverts extra water in the direction of summer- cultivated melon fields nearby whenever it rains.

Animals--mostly geese--are not permitted in the swimming pond because they have their own watering pond fenced away from the main Promenade between the Cloister and Highway 692 where they roam along the outer boundary.

Backing up to Elder Apartments is the same Clubhouse--where we came in--built as any public clubhouse, a solid brick facing on insulated concrete, with decks, for many different uses. It serves the whole community in many ways having to do with caring for the Very aged, the very young, and new Villagers just having moved in. They is also a very powerful political and labor Presence.

Elders are likely to show up as advocates just about anywhere in the Village.

Oh! here comes Jake Tailor. "Hey Jake! How ya doin'?"

"Just gittin' picture tacks. They're all in a hurry over there."

"For what?"

"I dunno. . . . Who's this you got witcha?"

"Oh, just a visitor--"

Jake interrupts--"Let me tell you something right now, son! Being in a hurry doesn't get you anyplace at all. Now, you listen ta me . . . while I tell you a story." And Jake continues:

"A philosophy professor stands before his class with some stuff on the table in front of him. When class begins, without a word he picks up a large empty canning jar and proceeds to fill it with rocks about 2-½ in diameter.

"He then asks the students if the jar is full? And they agreed that it is.

"So the professor picks up a box of pebbles and pours them into the jar. He shakes the jar lightly, so the pebbles, of course, roll into the open spaces between the rocks. He then asks the students again if the jar was full.

"They agree it is. The students laugh. The professor picks up a box of sand and pours that into the jar. Of course, the sand fills up everything else.

"'Now', says the professor, 'I want you to recognize that this is your life. The rocks are the important things - your family, your partner, your health, your children - things that if everything else was lost and only they remained, your life would still be full. The pebbles are the other things that matter--like your job, your house, your car. The sand is everything else, the small stuff.

"If you put sand (the small stuff) into the jar first, there is no room for pebbles or rocks. The same goes for your life. If you spend all your time and energy on the small stuff, you never have room for the things that matter.

"Pay attention to the things that matter to you. Play with the kids. Take time to be healthy. Take your partner out dancing. There will always be time to go back to work, clean the house, and fix the disposal.

"Take care of the rocks first - the things that really count. Set priorities. The rest is just sand'"

But then I pipe in, ... "I bet you could still pour in some beer and the jar wouldn't be so full that it couldn't contain beer! The beer would fill in the remaining spaces in the jar, and then it would be truly full."

And Jake says, "Yeah, I guess that's right. There's always room for beer! See you 'round!" And off he goes.

Past the Elders Apartments, you will not see any other houses because permanent tipis, campers and trailers have mounds spaced between for peace and quiet.

Residents here who have not yet attained their own permanent homes still are situated for privacy and convenience as volunteers and parents of children, whether adopted, foster or biological.

Pyramid-geo-homes are terraced into the ground so all you see from a distance is the glazed greenhouse. Access is not a problem because paths separate and encircle everything, and every resident has carts and bicycles.

Anyone in the Village who has a car parks it permanently at the Carpool. But what you the Visitor can see is only hedgerows, landscaped berms, greenhouses, eight permanent public buildings (Clubhouse, Retreat Building, Cistern Platform, Voc Tech, Sharing School, Library-Rotunda, Co-Op and Motor Pool), gardens (and tents) in the summer and mulched planting beds or snow-laden mounds in the Winter.

That's our goal, to be as nearly invisible as possible to the naked eye, at a distance and by satellite. You scatter eight permanent buildings and some greenhouses over a thousand acres, and yes, we're blending in pretty well.

Life Care

Everybody "exits" just as everybody "exists," At some point in life, the thought of death enters. It enters as accident, disease or intention. The intention to exit is visible as an indicator--that of emptying oneself of commitments, belongings and cares. When a person is no longer "engaged," that is the time to move them into Elder Housing, where coasting and boasting are the days' primary activities. But, life passes on and the funeral becomes a reality for the rest of us to deal with.

We know that morbid infectious illnesses exists all over the world. Here, terminal disease that is infectious is dealt with according to laws of Fairness--that is to say--the Safety of the Villages takes precedence over preferences of residents. If keeping the Village safe from morbid disease means that village brothers need to move a family to one of our other villages serving as a way station for the afflicted, then that is what occurs. The family is moved, but they only keep what can be washed and sanitized. Everything else--including the house itself--is burned down and consumed by fire.

Then, on arriving at their new Village, they will be supplied with all their needs from sanitary stores.

Among the still-engaged Elders are a couple of experts in classical languages, a storyteller, a librarian, potter, the ornithologist, two different kinds of solicitor/attorney and several teachers. Many of them have relinquished prestige and advantage to come live here specifically because they wanted to live a Simple Life.

This Village operates on principles of a Simple Life. Let me explain. In primitive societies, it is necessary for the people to keep moving just to obtain the things that make their lives adequate. People who travel are in the position to share, to trade, to barter whatever skills and material things they happen to have. But we are immobilized here. We have stopped traveling, so the opportunities for us to trade and barter are diminished. Can you see how that must make a difference in the amount of Stuff we can obtain?

Voluntary Simplicity is another way of saying voluntary poverty. We're all agreed here that Stuff is Not Important; it's People (and our animal friends) who are important. Yet we must appear to you to be relatively impoverished. But to our Way of thinking, it is the people who merely obtain things who are impoverished. Our lives are rich With each other, and you city people can just keep all your nice things.

The universe is filled with every kind of people. It can be said we live in a world which is materially rich and spiritually poor. We, like monks and nuns everywhere who have taken vows of poverty--Old Order Amish and Quakers,

Twelve Tribes, Buddhist and Ananda Marga monks--are materially poor and spiritually rich.

We pride ourselves in being this way. We boast about our poverty. Our time and our spaces are our own. No one tells us what to do or when to do it. We have no obligations to any worldly obligations, and yet each of us is also free to pursue our own interests and deal with the outside in any way that does not disrupt the Village. Yet the personal cost of our lives is very high, and we have to utilize our intelligence to survive. Most of us do not have money to smooth the Way and make it easy. Life is not easy here; but it's interesting.

Enough lecturing, let's get going.

* * * * *

What is commonly called a Nursing Home we call Heaven's Door. It's the last building you'll be able to see from the path before we get back to the main road and parking lot. In a wheel-shaped configuration like Sharing School, a single large geo-dome center with five abutting multi-level glazed pyramids, we care for chronically ill and dying members of our community with their families present. There are twelve beds in six special rooms, and either two or three nurses on staff at all times, plus family members who help out.

If a person is confused or de-evolved, s/he is led to a solitary plain room where s/he may fast and pray for Clarity for 60 hours. At the end of that time, if they're still mentally incompetent, they are taken by Med Unit to a hospital on the outside for assessment, treatment or custodial care.

Because our Village operates without cash money, what is certain is a resident who must be taken outside to a hospital will become subject to the charity hospital system; so we do everything we can to avoid that contingency.

During the hours of night when everyone is sleeping and few calls for advice reach the Door, nurses on duty are in the Nursing Wing, reading to the sleepless, massaging and bathing those who are suffering; rocking a sick child to sleep; or massaging their feet. For one who is preparing to Go Home, nurses help each member of the family to say good-bye and facilitate everyone's acceptance of the coming separation; serve refreshments, or do whatever else may be appropriate. In no case are patients simply left to suffer through uncomfortable or sleepless nights, or to be drugged to sleep.

Diversity prides itself in a holistic approach to health, because that approach means the people love each other; and they're not distracted by technology from cuddling and comforting their family members.

Diversity loses a resident to death now and then; and we have our own mortician, Lennie Duggan, coming to Heaven's Door and helping us deal with details and problems associated with maintaining sanitation this occurs. Most members opt for cremation and an urn memorial in Founders' Wall on the village plaza. Come on. Let's go get a cup of coffee.

I want to show you something.

Community Holy Days, by Season

There are six major Village Holy days in the Village, according to the Solar year. Each Holy day Festival takes up three days in which all formal schedules are forgiven, and everybody just pitches in as they happen to feel like it. Usually everybody feels like it because Festivals are a great deal of fun and activity.

SPRING

Spring Equinox is important for adapting to and promoting new Life in every way. It has been noted that human babies born in the Winter get the best cuddling, so spring is a good time to start a new baby. It is also time for starting new growth of all kinds. Some activities which are included in the three days of Spring Equinox are:

* Building new pyramid greenhouse/apartments,

* planting new perma-culture fields hedged by brier patches

* establishing new orchards with temporary greenhouse conditions;

* having a seed, survival tools and book swap and

* announcing engagements

To prepare for the Spring Equinox, the Greenhouse makes certain abundant supplies of Greens are sprouting and growing, so that the Village can retire their reliance on Grains and Staples and adopt a Spring diet of Greens, berries, and dried fruits, to clean out the Body and Get Moving again. As usual, meat is served only on the Sabbath.

Since children are in school during the winter, the focus of many of their school projects has been on biology and initiating life and growth.

PENTACOST

Pentecost is held on the weekend closest to May 15th. It is a three-day Festival which honors an individual Branch of Spirit each year, in 7-year cycles.

Invitations are sent out to the Governing Body or Conference of a cluster of churches each Spring, to invite them to come share their Traditions with the village. The Festivals are listed as:

~The Festival of Charismata,
~The Festival of Evangelism,
~The Festival of Angels,
~The Festival of Anabaptists,
~The Festival of Liturgies,
~The Festival of Peace, and
~the Founders' Festival every seven years.

Choral groups come from all over to invoke the Holy Spirit in song and prayer.

Spring is also the time for courting, working on a future and planning a wedding. Just as in the world there are "quick" weddings, "family" weddings and "church" weddings, we have the same custom. Except we go deeper.

A quick wedding is one in which the bride and groom have not known each other very long; their families are absent; and they are marrying for relative convenience, companionship and an opportunity for sexual expression.

Any ordained, certificated official may perform the ceremony; and usually the couples friends put together a potluck supper before the couple goes on their away-trip. Other cultures call this sort of wedding a "hand-fasting."

Separation and divorce is not an uncommon outcome; but the time spent in that relationship that was deep and intimate is seen to have been beneficial experience.

The "Church" wedding is one in which the bride and groom have known each other briefly, and what they have in common is their faith. So, they take ministerial classes in wedded bliss, and then their minister performs a ceremony "til death do us part."

Sometimes that "takes," and sometimes it does not. Children are usually born to these unions; and they make up about half our children at Sharing School--the half of children born to young parents who are less likely to have the patience to be truly good parents. But hopefully, their church guides them in the right way.

But our "Family" weddings are different. These marriages arise among the families of orphaned and abandoned children whose parents came here in midlife and established a home, a culture, a way of being in the world that they then taught to their adopted children. They mentor their children, they role-model patience and forbearance, they show their children what a deep and profound (usually late) marriage consists of.

And they bring their children to the altar to marry as virgins, so that the bond of marriage is final as the pair bond between snow geese is final. When two families-by-affinity bring their virginal children to the altar to marry, the whole village and visitors from all over show up to bless this union that would have been impossible except by the Grace of God and the help of the angels. And these are celebrations indeed. Simple, elegant, and involving a Ceremony and a noisy Send-off, there is no big feast, just a Cake and tea so all gifts go into making the new bride and groom as comfortable as can be in their new home.

SUMMER

The Summer Solstice is a busy time. Village farmers and gardeners need assistance with cultivating and planting. There's a lot of physical work to do, and the village must support the people who work hard by feeding them physically and spiritually. This is a time for building endurance; so dancing and athletic events (for FUN, not for winning) are held at the Summer Solstice Festival.

Food served to residents starting from the Summer Solstice leaves aside the greens and berries of Spring and adapts to fruits and vegetables in season as well as sprouted grains, nuts and seeds, and dairy products instead of meat.

Of course, soy milk, tofu and flat breads are available all year long, 365 days a year.

Christians adapt to the diet that they adapt to, and no compulsion is placed upon them to follow the Law with respect to diet, because they are justified by faith in and out of respect for the sacrificed blood of Jesus.

After the Solstice, residents will coordinate their 10-day vacations or business travel or trade shows or conventions or retreats until harvest-time, when food gathering and preservation needs to be completed by anyone in the village affected by presence or absence of food stores (in other words, those in the Village who AbideWith Favor and live without money).

AUTUMN

Fall Equinox is a time of Thanksgiving for another bountiful Year-of-yields. For us this season is the end of a productive year; and the oncoming winter will be utilized in meetings to plan for the next year's crops and activities, based on the richness of this bounty just harvested.

It's a special time of acknowledging the gifts our pyramid technology has conferred on us as a people; and it's a time when we all go outdoors to assist ingathering of apples, gourds and pumpkins we grow outside; grains and nuts and the seeds we husband so carefully. We must bale up lots of forage for our animal friends; gather up, chip and mulch stalks and vines for soil-building; lead the pigs from one harvested site to the next to scour plants and weeds out of the soil prior to mulching.

Fall is a time for us to prepare the ground for winter so our short outside growing season next year will also be bountiful as possible in the space we have.

Thanksgiving Festival comprises a three-day Gathering in which everyone shares his or her bounty with everyone else. Everyone gives and everyone receives their needs in return. One might compare the Gathering as a giant flea market and gift exchange. Its purpose is to Make Money Moot. Everybody shows up because they want to profit from God's Grace which is distributed at the Gathering. You'll hear more about this later, when we tell you more about the blue and white striped Gathering Tent and how we use it to encourage people to share what they have, what they know and what they can do FOR each other.

As the finale of the last In-Gathering, all Tents are taken down for the winter season. All Pavilions are laid bare so only geo-homes, churches, the Laundry, the Co-op, the Hospital and our Schools are left to withstand winter's weathering. All tents and extra trailers are warehoused safely out of sight.

From the Fall Equinox onward, we're eating breads with nuts and seeds (for extra energy), squashes, pumpkins, gourds, potatoes and apples, since most of the fruits are no longer in season. Some dried fruits and preserved berries are good, but it is expensive to try to sustain oneself on them. Meat is appropriate, so long as the animal has not died of deprivation or disease.

After the Gathering, everyone gets busy fulfilling Pledges they made at the Gathering. Women make winter wear out of wool and cotton fabrics that the Community weaves or gets in trade. It's time to start battening down for the winter. At this time, the Community turns Inward and observes a Formal Thanksgiving, each Resident in his or her new Formal Coatings and Accessories.

All disputes are brought to the Elders for Resolution. All Babies born during the year are Christened and given Formal Names. Engagement Plans and School Plans are recognized and moves are made to adapt to Change.

People leave, some temporarily and some permanently.

There's a lot of inner work to be done in the winter : manufacture of warm clothing for use and sale is our primary non-farm business, and this business is one that encourages silence and contemplation. Also, any excesses we achieve in growing food in our greenhouses are dehydrated and packaged. So winter is a very busy time for us. There is a slacking off of the physical so we can attend to the Subjective.

This is a good time to share with your our orientation to the metaphysical. While our members are in a lot of different mental spaces, the process by which we grow and develop psychically, mentally and spiritual is what we have in common.

From earliest childhood, children have been taught how to attend to, note and record physical attributes and indicators. That's just school, including the ability to hear at a distance, see at a distance well enough to make discriminations about movement, discriminate by smell and get along in the dark.

At the same time, children are learning by associating and cohering with a group, relating, role-playing, to lead, to follow, to get out of the way, to approach, to avoid, to conceal oneself, to confront openly, to speak one's truth clearly. None of our children turns out to be passive aggressive or passive resistant because skills and tools to deal with reality are mastered in school, or the child decides to go do something else, outside. Straight on, kids are given to understand that sexuality carries heavy penalties and responsibilities, so they learn to put it off.

So, we work from the physical into the social, and then we watch what they do with it. A child who is socialized early and whose parents can predict what is black for them and what is white for them is in a favored situation.

"Coming up with a new idea" becomes the favored behavior, and interpreting where that idea comes from becomes the challenge of the parent or teacher. Naturally, we teach the children by role-modeling the process of journaling that putting ideas to work means you have to write them down first and save them until they can be useful--some time in the future.

But even before a kid is literate, they have new ideas we must assess and access the subjective Source. Winter time is when we mostly have time, because we're carding or weaving (mechanically) or quilting or embroidering or pressing, to meditate over the ideas our children bring to us, and take a moment to record our interpretations, to move with or move over.

Just as bugs, bees and snakes are precious to God, our children's ideas are precious to us, even before they are practical. We trade in ideas the way that other people in the world trade in gossip. It's less harmful and intrusive to the personal ego, and it's just another form of entertainment when it's cold outside and our hands are busy inside.

WINTER

Winter solstice is a formal time of reflection. Perhaps it's also time for a new birth in the family, and the infant can be held and cuddled and kept snug and warm because there's really nowhere to go when the weather is harsh and cold.

Even though the jitney goes on its way as usual, its pace is more sober and deliberate; and it often goes 'on delivery' with a couple of extra hands to deliver the needs and staples of families on its way.

Or if one of the jitneys has broken down, we must then engage donkeys in the task of pulling supplies around to our residents. Usually a winter run takes longer because folks offer a hot drink or snack to the driver when he brings their bounty, so figure at least 90 minutes between runs from November through March.

After Winter Solstice, a few fresh foods are available with nuts and seeds sprouted at home and greens grown in greenhouses. Raisins and dried fruits provide some variety in a diet consisting largely of grains, beans, soups made from soup bones, dried vegetables, nuts and oil. Usually, little milk is available at this time, due to lack of fresh grass for goats and Dan's cows. But of course there's always plenty of fresh soy-milk, tofu, rice and flat-bread with seeds.

Solstice is family time. Sikhs are gone for a week, to their formal Solstice observances. Families decorate their homes and churches with pine boughs, popcorn and artwork from Sharing and VocTech schools; mothers stay busy making cookies and hot meals to deliver to those who are shut-in.

Dancers practice their steps; singers sing at supper with the choral director's urging. Teachers organize plays and sets and costumes and recitals so the village can see how all the children are progressing in life and knowledge and articulations.

Christians will observe Christmas and sing Carols; and Sikhs will observe an extended 10-day Solstice; Jews observe Hanukkah, and those who Abide with Favor spend time together with each other and make Music, Songs, and dance together for the sake of Love alone.

This is also a time for the Elders to Reflect on the State of the Village, on the progress of the Souls who have chosen This Way to live. It's a time to remove the names of those who have Gone On, to see a commitment to studying in earnest by those who are postulants to the Way, and to count up debits and credits on the balance sheet.

A verdict needs to be made whether the Community is growing too fast, not fast enough, or in fact shrinking and how to adapt to the Changes that arise. This is also an appropriate time for a 3-day Silent Retreat in order to hear the Will of God for the next calendar year.

Drama

Archetypes of village life are important Role Models for the villagers. The 'State of the Village' message which Elders give on the first Sabbath Blessing of a new solar year speaks to Growth and Development of village archetypes.

Role models residents adopt have nothing to do with spiritual practice. Our roles are constant features that hold and bind together all spiritual associations in the Village. We are not an ideological village. We are a functional cooperative, serving as a town.

At the amphitheater, plays are enacted that help the children visualize their own archetypes. Plays vividly portray angelic direction for archetypal growth.

Village meetings are arranged around the necessity for archetypal roles to interact, not just as occasions for friends to hob- knob personally around kinships and preferences.

The fact that archetypes exist makes life reflect Nature and keeps life interesting, but it also brings conflict. The purpose of Drama is to head-off conflicts between different ways of Perceiving Life, in the village.

It is expected that most residents will hang-out with their families most of their free time. If someone is absent from their family circle a great deal of the time, that is seen as a sign of impending Separation.

The Village's response to an impending Separation is to offer Visitation--to bring help to the remaining family members during their grieving period. While the dispute resolution process is under way, until the matters have resolve themselves and the family has adjusted to a New Way of Self-Sufficiency, visitations and assistance will continue under the headship of the Village Secretary.

Cycles of Life

Adapting oneself to the cycles of life is never a perfect science. Individuals TEND to progress from archetype to archetype about every seven years; they TEND to throw themselves into chaos when their archetype is no longer working appropriately.

People TEND to act out their inner conflicts BEFORE they can articulate what is really going on; and people TEND to marry the archetype of their Hated Parent and then proceed to grow AWAY from that archetype.

So, Village life has adapted itself to these Realities, and it provides opportunities for residents to grow into--and out of--many roles. Yet, the fact remains that an average of three families moves out of town each year; and an average of five new families moves in.

The way the Village handles an extra new family that wants to move in is to provide the family with a trailer space, a trailer, and some work experience, and see what happens.

They are Noticed by the Village until they know how to fit in.

Moving IN & OUT

Handling those who need to leave is simple, but it is not easy. There are just a few circumstances which will bring the Elders to immediately expel a resident from the community: violence, theft, and chaos [gossip].

If a man leaves a mark on a woman or child; impregnates a woman not his wife; or betters another man in a fight, the brothers take him to the garage and present him with a specially-painted black and white striped car, $100 in cash, one suit of clothes. They escort him to the Entrance to the Village, and call the local State Police to inform them that this person is no longer welcome in the Community.

He must be exiled for a year; and then if he makes supplication and agrees to make amends and restitution, then he may return. If, on the other hand, he actually maims another person, he is remanded over to the Authorities.

Victims of crimes of violence often unwitting contribute to their own undoing. Therefore, the Elders Notice them, and bring them to attention of mature women of reputation, to ascertain the extent and depth of their lack of self-esteem.

Over the period of a year, the Village does whatever it can to restore a Victim to his/her self of Oneness with God; but if that does not work, then the person is referred to another Place to live.

Other Residents will leave the Village when their Role no longer fits and they cannot imagine themselves adopting a New Village archetype; they will leave when a conflict disrupts their sense of Belonging; they will leave when circumstances over which they have no control force them to leave; and they will leave because Evil turns them from the Path of Integrity. There's no use Judging Others because they leave or because they appear to cause others to leave. God is our Judge.

Archetypes of Village Life

Every person in the Village is needed for themselves. But it helps Diversity operate if the people understand Diverse Perspectives so they do not stumble over Diversity and mistake it for lack of Integrity. These are the people who make the Village WORK.

Indeed, no monastery or religious order needs a government agency to serve in headship over it. People who are inner-directed do not need supervision or rules to tell them what to do. Thus, this community finds "gubmint" to be not only superfluous, but also excessive and tyrannical, by definition.

This listing is different from the one given for a Devotional Community. In a diverse village, people are expected to tolerate a broader spectrum of individual differences than in a religious brotherhood.

In the village there is a labor group for each professional arche-type; and it serves for all residents regardless of personal religious or political ideology. These groups comprise the GLUE that hold this Village together--not ideology, not spiritual leadership, not a One Way view of God-given existence.

Archetype 1. Culturally-isolated right-Brain dominant Sensor : Assistant, Baker, Cook, Construction worker, Firefighter, Laborer, Road Crew, Warehouseman. --

These individuals take orders, keep order and provide stamina to the community because they want to fit in. Most of them work in or near the Promenade because that's where THEIR friends are; they want to be together all the time in any case. Most are actually very shy private (usually young) people who still socialize in a very stylized way and avoid diverse people. That's how they are identified, by their avoidances.

The way the village motivates new and young members is to give them access to three square meals, the gym, spa and salon, barber shop and movie lounge with some new clothes and a clean room of their own. With a short 4-hour work shift to qualify for these perks, they're quite happy to comply if they really want to be here. On the other hand, if this is not an acceptable deal, they clearly don't want to be here. Simple, no?

Once having mastered the ability to focus, listen and take orders, they work on establishing limits and boundaries of what is safe and appropriate in the community to which they want to belong.

Then, having mastered what is appropriate, they set about to solve problems where they are until they move into ONE OF the THREE comprehensive specialties every villager must master : gardening, recycling or health sciences.

Archetype 2. Culturally isolated left-brain dominant Sensor. -- Horticulturist, rancher, farmer, field hand, gardener, groundsman, harvester, housewife, housekeeper, Re-cycler.--

Caring for land and/or animals and perceiving real problems, these promote life and hate waste. Many of them work long hours because they have young burgeoning families with burgeoning needs.

Archetype 3. By now socialized to be safe, appropriate, tolerant, as well as experienced in a field of their choice, these individuals "make things nice for" people -- Blacksmith, Butcher, Foreman, Housewife, Helper, Horse Trainer, Inspector, Launderer, Lumberman, Presser.

Adapting what is natural to the needs of others, they do or make things to adapt to Diversity of needs. They never stop trying to "get it right." They are often young and must be confronted over working on the Sabbath because they forget what day it is.

Archetype 4. Socialized Tolerant "make things work for" people. Mechanic, Programmer, Repairman, Salvage Operator, Smith, Tool maker, Truck driver. -- These reckon rules and adapt the environment to the people. They try to follow everybody else's rules, so they are busy all the time because "somebody has to follow all the rules." Extra "credit" they accrue gives them a feeling of security. As aged adults, they are adored by their apprentices and prized by their old customers.

Archetype 5. Idealist right-brain-dominant athletes, they reckon which rules they are willing to follow. -- Athlete, Carpenter, Bricklayer, Dancer, Instructor.

These individuals provide the village with vitality. They usually split their time between school (teaching or learning) and their craft. Always cheerful and outgoing, as they get on in years, quite often they move into the work of direct caring--for the needs of the sick or dying.

Archetype 6. Idealist left-brain talkers. -- Activist, Actor, Barker, Clerk, Customer Rep, Choral Director, Officer, Operator, Patrolman, Singer, Ticket-taker, Tour Guide -- These individuals provide the Village with Cheer and Harmony because they "wanna tell folks how it is"--especially having to reckon rules in a rule-bound culture. Splitting their time between helping others and with-drawing into their own private (contradictory) needs, these needed management trainees.

A village requires four shifts of four officers and four shifts of three nurses to run the Needs Center and the Clinic 24/7. Officers supervise grounds men and provide assistance to any resident with a problem who calls in. (Remember, we are isolated away from city services here.) They deliver babies and calves, bring children down out of trees, attend to injured and transport them to the Clinic, mediate disputes, and--of course--help find what or who is Lost. The service station helpers and customer servers are Officers in training.

As an aside, there are also two choral directors in our village, one who works with anyone in the community wanting to learn Rounds and one who teaches Piano and

Violin. They each accept apprenticeships and teach one group class per day. The rest of their time is spent on practicing the technical mastery of the craft; but they will express their feelings and emotions as the group's music.

Archetype 7. Idealistic intuitive doers -- Florist, Poet, Secretary, Steward, Stone worker. -- These individuals bring Clarity and Definition or Beauty to the village. They are people whose difficult situations or temperaments make it difficult for them to be centered all the time; so they learn to work through the Dark Side with hard physical (or mental) labor and to come out on the other side with insights and clarity in the form of sculpture, literature, order & organization, poetry, recitation or art.

Archetype 8. Contemplative intuitives.-- Potter -- Maker of baskets, bowls, boxes, bricks, cabinets, caskets, dishes, furniture, glasses and windows.

These individuals promote order and containment. Reticent and orderly by nature, they are disturbed by others' noise and mess and driven to provide ways to keep things neat. They want to contain the whole world in comfort. They want everything to match and will go to great pains to make things that do. They are ceaseless workers because there is always "one more thing to do."

Archetype 9. Problem-solving intuitives (quiet types). They deal with multiple progressions and sequences of steps and modes. Construction super, electrician, inventor, metal fabricator, plumber, seamstress, tailor.

Quite often very intelligent people (with difficult histories) with good memory, and they may consider themselves to be inarticulate for some reason and pour themselves into their craft as compensation. Or, they're subjectively disturbed at times, so they alternate between solitude and very focused work and some limited sociability. Problems drive creative doers.

Archetype 10. Problem-solving articulators (talkers)--Instructor, healer, manager, monk, mortician, salesman, supervisor, teacher trainer.

These individuals deal with the need to control. These are the individuals who have come from great suffering in the past, and they are working out their salvation with fear and trembling. They work double-shifts, and they are afraid to account fully for their time or their money.

These hand down access to tools, information, and skill. Their minds never stop figuring out how to control things in a better way, and they themselves will work as two or three different archetypes in any given Day. They will only Rest when they know that everyone else is working. On the sabbath, they work hard at resting because they never put their ideas down.

Archetype 11. Predators -- Accountant, Attorney, Composer, competitive craftsman, entrepreneur, legislator, mafia. Yes predators are a necessary part of life. They create and cull excesses. Behind the scenes, sometimes they appropriate excesses for themselves (called profits). They are masters of facts and information for decision-making. Predators have a thin veneer of sociability; but their real interest is power that information provides.

Managing and motivating truth-full 'bean counters' is a challenge of any administrator because--competent or incompetent, honest or not--they all have a very pleasant, disarming demeanor--highly socialized--and they can create rules-upon-rules and make it appear fair even when it's not fair. Competition drives strategizing.

The way ethical predation is done is by refining an art or gift into such excellence that it surpasses all other artistic expressions of the day and a demand is created. That is the way great music occurs, by composers wanting to surpass and overwhelm other composers' works.

When predators themselves multiply in order to endanger whole populations (as in genocidal and omnicidal Fascist corporations) that's when our prayers for deliverance make a difference. God needs to hear when predation has become excessive. "Defense industries" are an example of excessive predation; so are "biological weapons" and "nuclear waste."

Archetype 12. Supervisors & Directors -- Administrator, Chaplain, Coordinator, Executive, Magician, Minister, Monarch, Priest, Principal.

These are usually smarter than the predators they confront because they understand [by Holy Spirit] truth, compassion, mercy, limits on liberty by dominion and sovereignty. Liberty is all we ever get, who live here, as individuals. As a community we assert dominion over our property. As for Sovereignty, it belongs to God alone. We find that, when an executive or monarch slips into predation, it is because they have already wasted themselves, first.

Directors make things happen which need to happen. Sometimes they are abrupt and abrasive, sometimes they don't have enough facts to back up their judgments, sometimes they do not truly listen to the people they must direct. Yet, their Integrity lies in the Way they learn to be open with people, to establish strong Expectations, and to work consistently and fairly with the same people year in and year out.

Archetype 13. Subjective & Objective coordinators -- Village Secretary, aide, bus driver, volunteer, guide, helper.

These individuals are open to listening to and coordinating needs for the New, the Young, the Sick, the Old and those who are physically vulnerable for any reason. They are always open to Others; so they are also always at the point of burning out. Christian helpers are centered and helpful because they have taken on the suffering of the Christ and His brothers as their own. That is their operative strategy : "Do unto others."

Archetype 14. Subjective & Objective synthesizers. -- Guru, Master, Prophet, Rabbi -- The actual leader of this place is responsible to God--as Adam, Noah, Abram and Moses were--for the condition and circumstances of his flock, for the correct understanding of Holy Law.

Effects, results and outcomes that Holy Law portray and manifest are the subject of this individual's work and learning. Totally effects oriented, the 'mayor" of the village attacks and corrects processes and procedures with abandon and outrage when these don't work out.

Preferences or Attachments.

What this list comes down to, once you realize it is a natural progression, is that there is a natural movement from effort to happiness if one follows spirit and does not live in denial and avoidance. That natural progression goes like this: The natural process of success and manifestation never operates under compulsion, under threat, in times of danger, in times of worry or great stress.

Indeed, auras of worried people are very dark, and they are not seen easily by angels. This is why God's people are told to throw all their cares upon Him, to free their spirits.

At the End : a Funeral

We as a community have built this our Village with our own hands. When someone leaves us to Go Home To God, we agree that this person will never be far from us because we have lived together and lacked together and adapted together in Life. Thus, it is appropriate that each one who dies should keep his or her place of honor in our Village, in death.

Lenny Duggan, the mortician on duty, is fully licensed to do all kinds of funerals; and it is true that sometimes Christian and Autonomous families hold more strongly to their doctrines than they do to our Village. But we DO HAVE traditions associated with death and dying, so it has become an orderly practice.

When a person dies, our practice is that after 12 hours of stillness and cooling, they are cremated in a bonfire and the ashes are placed in a solid rock geo-sphere made of two interlocking hemispheres that are hollow on the inside. This rock geo-sphere, each one weighing about 3 pounds, is taken out of storage and fitted into the solid rock wall of the Formal Garden [near Senior Apartments] just as soon as we need that wall to be further built upon.

And then once a year the 'face' of this rock is polished and names of this year's deceased are chiseled into the rock wall [similar to the Viet Nam War Memorial in Washington, D.C.]. We need our land for our living, not for our departed, which now number only three, two elderly and one young dancer, Molly.

Placement of stone urn is done during a Remembrance Service, and each family specifies who will conduct the Remembrance and how many people they can suffer to attend. There will also be a lower retaining wall of the Formal Garden for cremated remains of our Sentinel Corps and family pets. So far, none of these have died.

The personal effects of a deceased [clothes, shoes, linens--few in number if s/he died in advanced age] are placed in a basket and burned at the Remembrance Service, as part of letting go of their role and place in community.

More durable items--jewelry, housewares--are distributed as the deceased person's Journals specify. In Molly's case, she left nothing because she was adopted at age six; and nobody knew she had (presumably) a heart problem (she collapsed in the gym) until it was too late.

The deceased resident's journals serve as their legal last will and testament. They will be kept in the Library "until no one can remember who they were." That way, villagers can remain in touch with the thoughts of their loved ones for a long, long time.

Molly's journal is read aloud in school all the time by the students who were her companions.

The Final Loop

Setting out on the fourth (North) Loop we pass by the Needs Center and head north past the Library, and then the Laundromat and Beauty Parlor are next, on the right before we get to the corporation yard where we keep construction materials, rock and sand.

If you would like to walk on up there and see those facilities, I'll give you a Spa Pass so you can relax and clean up before dinner. Want to?

The need to conserve waterlines, sewage lines, electricity, heat and labor has resulted in the decision to build a common laundry facility so all homes will not need to invest in a great deal of power and plumbing. The Village is implementing this decision also as a way to improve and encourage residents to share time together in good spirit, regardless of the mundane nature of the task at hand. Laundry is a mundane task, so why not make fun out of it? And we do.

The Jitney delivers people and dirty wash to the Laundromat. Some people volunteer to do a 4-hour shift each week, do their own wash, helping out others by sorting or folding, and get some credit for it. Others just drop theirs off (and let someone else do it) and walk down to the co-op or get their hair henna-ed or braided next door.

Still others watch children playing in the campgrounds' play area while their mothers' wash is washing. There are always choices to make, to keep Life interesting.

There are 24 Camp spaces in Cookie Circle (about 63 acres in size)--not just squares of dirt; each one is a raised platform (for a tent or tipi) that has an attached (discreet) loo and storage unit.

There is a large Bath House at the back of the Laundry Building, divided by sex, with plenty of soap, hot water and elbow room for people to use to clean things up.

There's a tot-wading pool, some swings and a campfire circle, and the campground itself is high enough in elevation it overlooks fields and trees beyond the village perimeter, so it doesn't feel cramped up there.

Kicking Back

Circling around on your right, you can see a small Retreat Lodge and Chapel that was built by Benedictine Brothers. It's set up to accommodate twelve monks in the Retreat House, and it has a separate Chapel for Eucharist or Mass, depending on who is sponsoring an event.

Village History

When the Founders originally acquired this property, they had funds to jump-start the Village's basic functions. In addition to putting-in Village Trail and all the water systems at once at the beginning, they also bought about 60 trailers--double-wides for Public functions and single ones for families--from Government surplus that have been utilized as Temporary Business and Housing here and there, as the Village has built up.

Nowadays, the only remaining trailers--small family sized ones like mine--are found here in Cookie Circle, still being utilized by new families from the time they arrive until a permanent house is freed up for them.

Coming back from the Chapel grounds, it is not yet built; the Gardens alone have been utilized for weddings in the summer and as a quiet Space for people to meditate. Yet, the feeling among the Residents is that, since our whole Way of Life is built on being Receptive to God's Leading, that adding one more space for Church services is necessary for our Residents who Abide By Law (Favor).

Public prayer is practiced at all village meetings; and Thanksgiving is returned on every Saturday Sabbath in each home; yet there has not been a place for Jews, Angels, the 7th Day Adventists, Twelve Tribes or Sikhs to keep their Sacred Books.

We visualize the Chapel as the Place For What Is Sacred : Silence, Study and Sacraments. There is a series of meetings of the Residents at this time, to define the Mission and Scope of the Chapel, and to begin the process of deciding what it will look like, how many Spiritual groups want to participate in its design and formation and what likely resources may come forward to promote its completion.

What is likely is that the building will be constructed of quarried stone, as our amphitheater is constructed, and that it will be built around a central geodesic Dome-Atrium combination. We'll have to see what turns up.

Diversity is a play about the future of our planet--IF our planet is going to have a future. Due to the fact that human lifestyles either function in harmony with its eco-system or serves to deplete, exhaust, and destroy its world, God has dictated this account of Life in the material as a model for a human Future.

It has been presented as an abundant picture of Life in the future as a narrated play and mental picture book so children will understand it easily and will be able to act it out on stage, in different settings but with the underlying message of Hope for something better that it brings.

This is the end of the play. Now, let's go make it happen.

Oh Most Merciful God, give us the Wisdom, the Insight and the Tact, to unseat Evil, preempt Deceit, and mitigate micro-management and thought controls. Indeed, we are your Free Spirited Children. Amen.

www.ingramcontent.com/pod-product-compliance
Lightning Source LLC
Chambersburg PA
CBHW030421290526

45786CB00001B/77
* 9 7 8 1 5 3 0 8 1 3 0 9 4 *